STEAMING IN

STEAMING IN

The Classic Account of Life on the Football Terraces

COLIN WARD

**SIMON &
SCHUSTER**

London · New York · Sydney · Toronto · New Delhi

A CBS COMPANY

First published in Great Britain by Simon & Schuster UK Ltd, 1989
This paperback edition published by Simon & Schuster UK Ltd, 2013
A CBS COMPANY

1 3 5 7 9 10 8 6 4 2

Simon & Schuster UK Ltd
1st Floor
222 Gray's Inn Road
London WC1X 8HB

www.simonandschuster.co.uk

Simon & Schuster Australia, Sydney
Simon & Schuster India, New Delhi

Every reasonable effort has been made to
contact copyright holders of material reproduced in this book.
If any have inadvertently been overlooked, the publishers would
be glad to hear from them and make good in future editions
any errors or omissions brought to their attention.

A CIP catalogue record for this book
is available from the British Library

ISBN: 978-1-47112-604-8
Ebook ISBN: 978-47112-605-5

Typeset in the UK by M Rules
Printed and bound by CPI Group (UK) Ltd, Croydon, CR0 4YY

To my Father
A great man and a
football fan

Contents

'You wanted combat for what?
I don't know really why.
Or really know why.
Who wants true combat? But here it is'

Ernest Hemingway
Across the River and into the Trees

Preface to the New Edition

Football is the beautiful game and nothing will ever change that, despite all the ballyhoo and hype that now surrounds every utterance from both fans and players, and the arrival of the super-rich, who want to nail their money to the football mast. Perhaps it didn't seem beautiful when the hooligan was in his pomp during the 1970s and early 1980s, the period described in this book. Many observers called us and the game itself ugly, but for the armies of fans who lived for Saturday afternoon at three o'clock and hero-worship of their team, it wasn't just the beauty of the game that drew us. It was more than that: it was our way of life, and our reason for getting up and going to work on Monday.

The twenty-year period when the terrace terrors were steaming in across England and Europe, and were accused of degrading and destroying the beautiful game, feels like a distant memory now. All the havoc we created sometimes seems tame compared with what we read about every week. Once it was the fans who were rampaging; today it seems as if every other footballer is taking drugs, getting into fights or assaulting women

after a night on the tiles. Money and greed beyond most footballers' wildest dreams are destroying the game faster than we
ever could, with our Laurel and Hardy punch-ups and pitch
invasions. Football violence, like all youth cultures of the post-
war era, had a lifecycle, and most hooligans grew up and moved
on. We didn't die, we just got old, and like returning soldiers
took our demob suit and put ourselves and our anger back
into line. It's now recognised that the change in football's culture was epitomised by Nick Hornby's bestselling book about
Arsenal, *Fever Pitch*, which seemed to be the announcement of
a new era, where nice people went to football and cheered their
team when they won and cried when they lost. No big television match is now complete without the camera zooming in on
some hapless losing fan consoling his girlfriend or younger
sibling as defeat becomes too much to bear. To me it was better
to get defeat out of your system by smacking some opposing
big-mouth in the teeth. Not to the guy who got smacked, perhaps, but as many teachers and those who fought a war often
used to remark – a good hiding never did anybody any harm.

The people in power were genuinely scared of a youth
movement that had no leaders and no allegiance except to
the cadre of friendship and their team colours. Perhaps,
inevitably, the cult of football hooliganism or 'designer violence' evolved into a fashion of sorts, causing politicians to
invest huge resources into undercover surveillance and intel-
ligence-gathering. After the Hillsborough disaster money
which football claimed it didn't have materialised in order to
build new all-seater stadiums, and the First Division became
the Premiership. Rupert Murdoch decided football was the
way forward for his dream of total media control, and suddenly the game was awash with money. Everybody wanted
to play in the English football league and foreign players
arrived by the dozen.

And now the terraces are no more, and the descendants of
the terrace terrors are being fleeced faster than a fleeing foot-

ball fan used to run. In many ways fans are now treated far worse than they ever were – at least we owned our little bit of crumbling concrete terrace, and the devil took the hindmost when we supported our team and defended our honour. We stuck two fingers up to everybody and punched any rival who insulted us. Now the power isn't even with the clubs, let alone the fans: it is Murdoch and his minions who decide which team plays where and at what time. The glitter and profits of television football have made superstars of players, who now earn hundreds of times the average industrial wage. When the miners went on strike for £100 a week in the 1970s, the top earners of the pre-Premiership First Division took home maybe ten times the average salary. Footballers used to travel home on the train with fans. After Arsenal drew with Stoke at Hillsborough in 1971 Ray Kennedy, later to win more medals than any other footballer, came home with my father and I on the London Underground, sporting a shiny black eye from a previous match at Blackpool.

Those were the days. Your team could be crap, but the First Division of fans was what really mattered. Newspapers used to report us as much as the match itself – legends were created in epic battles across crowded roads, railway lines, shopping centres and motorway service stations. Hearing the story of the toothless old-aged Millwall pensioner hanging out of her top window exhorting the Millwall hordes to 'go and do the Manc [Manchester] wankers' still makes me chuckle nearly forty years later. We loved that, and the thousands of other stories that surrounded us, and we loved the notoriety that went with it. Even now, just talking about what we survived is a bigger buzz than anybody can imagine, and very few people who lived through our experience feel bad about what we did.

While nobody really yearns for the return of the terraces – although the terraces themselves didn't cause hooliganism – the loss of the spontaneity of being able to attend a match as and when you felt like it has diminished the game. Our attendance kept many badly run clubs afloat, yet those in power rarely asked any football fan for their opinion or gave them the credence their fanaticism deserved. When they needed support, they asked the fans to cheer louder or pay more money for seats. Yet as soon as the fans got too worked up, they threw up their hands in horror. The funny thing was that in retrospect the power and influence we wielded was much greater than we realised.

Eventually the weight of the British state was brought to bear on the hooligan, and in the 1980s the world was treated to a series of show-trials initiated by the government of Margaret Thatcher. Friends of mine were tried and convicted on the basis of supposedly overheard conversations and then jailed for substantial periods. Many of these people were subsequently released after their evidence was found to be tainted and corrupt, eventually receiving substantial compensation from the government. Now the lads have all retired from active service and are busy writing their memoirs, but this is *Steaming In*, the book that started it all and the true story of what it was like to live a piece of history. Some of the participants in this book are no longer with us, but their memory will live on long after the new-money football fans have got bored.

When football violence does occasionally flare up at competitive high-pressure matches or local derbies, or Millwall have their annual bout of fisticuffs, the doom-mongers are quick to tell us that hooliganism is simmering away just below the surface, and if it weren't for the vigilance of the police, anarchy would return. The pictures of thousands of people wearing replica shirts tell another story, but what do the politicians care about the truth? It suited them to pillory us then, and it suits them now to use football as a cover for ulterior motives. Football has moved on from the terrace terrors, although the memory of our presence lingers.

And with each major international tournament, the memory resurfaces. It's all about reputation, as the past glories of the early travellers come back to haunt those England fans who travel to watch their team. The cult of English hooliganism is ever-present as foreign riot police simulate mock fights with people dressed as England fans. Getting battered by over-zealous police is seen as par for the course, with the assumption of provocation as the footage flashes across news channels around the world. Everyone tells you you're not welcome, when it just isn't true, and it fosters a no-one-likes-us-we-don't-care mentality. The British government has changed laws, removed fans' passports but still remains powerless to stop thousands of England fans descending upon foreign shores to enact an assault on foreign beer stocks. For some, the whiff of a confrontation still lingers, and they will cite it as the reason for going with a passion that would not disgrace Shakespeare's *Richard III*, even if the rhetoric of violence from forty- and fifty-something beer bellies outdistances the reality by some margin. Every major tournament is prefaced by discussion of what is laughingly . . . called the 'English disease', even if the copycat hooligans from Germany, Holland and now Turkey are far worse than England's fans – although it does always seem to be the English who start drinking at 8 a.m.

The game has changed, and *Steaming In* is now a picture of another era. Everybody is a spectator now, with some football grounds resembling a library reading room full of corporate clients eating their proverbial prawn sandwiches. But we were fans then, our passion and chanting a barometer of what we were. We didn't have happy childhoods: we had the football.

COLIN WARD
June 2013

1

Early Days

Somewhere, in a place called Utopia, is a football stadium which is covered all round, is all seated, and has a sheltered picnic area. Families go there on a Sunday afternoon with their best clothes on and watch football in reverential silence. These are matches in which nothing happens: nobody kicks each other or swears, and everyone plays the game for love, not money. Every week the stadium is packed and there is no booing, racism or fighting amongst the fans. When a goal is scored a polite ripple of applause breaks out. This is the Utopia of politicians who know virtually nothing about football and still less about football fans. Let me take you to the real stadiums among real football supporters – the guys who bust a gut to see their team and then get covered with water from a roadside puddle as the team coach shoots past with no acknowledgement of their support.

'Lend us ten pence, mate.' This was the catchphrase of the 'Ten-pence Tonys' who were a common sight on away-match days at main-line railway stations, cadging money to buy a train ticket. Once on the train they would patrol the carriages for ground entrance money, and the really cheeky ones would even go up and down the half-time food and drink queues for tea money. Nobody minded them for they seemed an essential part of away travel, and they always seemed to gain ground entry because most people chipped in – for their bare-faced cheek, I suppose. Sadly, the 'Ten-pence Tonys' are no more; nowadays the travelling fan will have plenty of money and the hooligan probably a stolen credit card. Every team had its 'Tonys', but in the early seventies Manchester United had a small army of them. The first time I encountered this phenomenon was at King's Cross railway station on a chilly March morning as I was preparing to travel to Sheffield for an FA Cup semi-final. I was confronted by two fearsome young black men wearing college-style Arsenal scarves. These weren't real 'Ten-pence Tonys' but chancers who saw me as an easy touch: I was only fifteen and distinctly nervous. I made an excuse and scurried into the buffet to look for my dad, with whom I was travelling to the match.

April 1970. The euphoria of the Fairs Cup win was over, and the real battle of the season was on: Spurs versus Arsenal. Did last week's victory count for anything? It didn't on the terraces, that's for sure, and I was to witness the excitement of terrace violence for the first time. Arsenal, my team, would take the Park Lane end. That is, Arsenal's young fans would invade the space that was the exclusive territory of Spurs supporters. Arsenal had the numbers and a desire to provoke a confrontation. I arrived at 2.15 p.m. and went on to the large side terrace called the Shelf which overlooks Park Lane. The Arsenal fans were in the Park Lane terrace chanting, 'Tottenham, where are you?'

At about 2.30 p.m. the Spurs fans arrived en masse and all hell broke loose. The Tottenham supporters surged on to the terraces and fists and boots started flying. I saw six fans beating the hell out of just one guy. If someone went down, the boot went straight in. The fighting was frantic and went on in sporadic outbursts for about five or six minutes until the police moved in. Just two or three quelled the rumpus, and strangely there were no bodies lying prostrate on the terraces. Sure, there would have been black eyes the next day, but nothing serious.

The Spurs fans had failed to dislodge the Arsenal supporters. They had gained some ground, but nothing dramatic. First blood to the Arsenal fans, who began chanting, 'We took the Park Lane.' In the second half Spurs scored a goal, whereupon Arsenal fans surged at the Tottenham supporters and more fisticuffs broke out. Again the police restored order, and this time they arrested a few of the protagonists.

The match finished – Spurs had won by one goal to nil – and the warring factions spilled out on to the High Road. The fighting ebbed and flowed, with terrified Saturday afternoon shoppers fleeing everywhere. Honours finished even, and although I went home feeling frightened I had seen enough to sense the feeling of excitement and to realise I wanted to be a part of it. The following year was to be the most successful for Arsenal, both on the pitch and on the terraces.

In the heyday of terrace violence, in the late sixties and early seventies, the fighting was fun, for the participants at least. In those days you were part of a real gang. There were no police escorts; in fact at some matches you never even saw a policeman. You had two options: stand and fight, or run for your life. It was obligatory to wear a scarf and was considered taboo to hide it when the going got rough, although a lot of people did just that. Once inside the ground you could walk right around and go in the home fans' end to invade their territory. Whether you did or not would depend upon your numbers and the reputation of toughness of the home fans. Every football ground had a popular end, and home fans would try to prevent rival fans entering it. If some did get through, then a punch-up usually ensued. Thus a new phrase entered the hooligans' vocabulary: 'taking an end'. If you got in and held your ground, you had 'taken' the end. Your manliness had been satisfied at the other fans' expense. Sometimes, though, you got chased right out – but it was all part of the experience. Of course, if your numbers were small then the home fans could walk round to you.

Travelling away could be a great experience or an appointment with fear. The best way to take an end was to mass at the top of the terrace and surge forward, punching and kicking all and sundry and causing everyone to scatter in panic. This was called 'steaming in'. In those days there were no organised gangs, just groups of football fans who were drawn together by the common love of the team and the excitement of the terraces. If you turned up and had the team colours then you were part of the gang. It mattered not one iota that you had never seen the guy standing next to you. If trouble started then you were expected to bail him out, and vice versa. It was an unwritten code, and you quite often became friends for the day, fighting buddies for two minutes. At the end of the day a 'cheerio' or 'good luck', then on your way. Sitting in a train carriage you had no idea whether the people you were teaming up with were cowards who would run at the first sign of trouble or raving lunatics who would want to pick fights against vastly superior numbers.

In those days the trouble was spontaneous and would usually erupt when one side scored a goal. Most fans get upset when a goal is scored against them, but for some the only remedy was to bust an opposing fan's nose. Of course, for many the football was incidental to the punch-up.

'Yeah, we had a great day out. Pissed as a rat, great knuckle and three of us got fined a tenner.'

'How did the match go?'

'Oh, we lost three–nil.'

Tall Eric, with his lean looks, quickfire patter and ability to command an audience, was a familiar face in the days before it was trendy to be well known. Everyone recognised and acknowledged him at Chelsea and he was once pictured in Club International modelling clothes outside a boutique in the King's Road. If anybody was responsible for bringing fashion on to the terraces, it was Eric. He would wear clothes that everyone else would be wearing six months later. Eric made his reputation at Chelsea by standing in a huge gap in the Shed and screaming 'Don't run, Chelsea' as the Chelsea fans scattered from the advancing West Ham hordes. Chelsea, thanks to Eric, held their ground and forced the West Ham supporters back.

Eric knew all the hard nuts at Chelsea, but he was not hard himself. It is very doubtful that Eric ever threw a punch before he retired from the terraces. He went to Birmingham one Bank Holiday afternoon in the early seventies wearing a white boiler suit and was immediately spotted by the Birmingham fans, who began to chant at him. Eric loved it, until it became obvious that Chelsea fans were not turning up in numbers that day. The Birmingham supporters waded into Chelsea, who ran everywhere, while poor Eric got cornered and took a real pasting. He even had a chunk of his boiler suit cut off by a young souvenir hunter. I never saw Eric at a football match again.

British Rail – what an institution! Inventor of the 'football special', in those heady days of the football excursion Awayday. It meant cheap travel, as much booze as you could consume and as many carriages as you could smash up in the course of the journey. If you vandalised a train really badly they would pull it in to a station and chuck you on to another train. British Rail even used to advertise in match-day programmes for the following week's cheap excursion train. There was half-price travel for those aged fourteen and under, and the number of people who fell into that age category was quite amazing – some of them six feet tall and with moustaches! The train would arrive and the fans spilled out of the carriages; if you were many, what a feeling! Station concourses are terrific places for chanting. There might be seven hundred people emerging from a train full of booze, hope and expectation. 'Arsenal, Arsenal' would echo through the high-roofed buildings, a crescendo of noise reverberating around the station. It used to deafen us and frighten the hell out of any poor soul who happened to be catching a train. We marched out of the station like young gladiators. If there was a mob waiting for us, then God help them if we were the hard nuts, and God help us if half our mob were runners. Mostly, though, a team turning up on a special had the ascendancy; their numbers were massed with a single objective.

It was after the match, when no one seemed to know where they were going, that everyone got split up and the home fans made their move; then the frightening time would start. There is usually a public house near a station, so the home hard nuts who fancied themselves would always try to put on a show when we turned up – standing outside drinking, trying to look flash. Mind you, they didn't look so flash when they dropped the beer and ran for dear life.

Sometimes it became necessary to remove your team colours and blend in with the locals if you were really out-numbered so that they would have to work out who was who. This was when the question 'What's the time, mate?' would come into use. After all, an accent gives away your origins immediately.

'What's the time, mate?'

'Oh, it's one-thirty' might be the reply, if you had the chance to finish. As soon as you spoke, though, you knew you had problems. 'You Cockney bastard' and a punch in the mouth usually followed, although not necessarily in that order. Rule number one: never go down, just keep running. When I got caught on my own – and it always happened – I tried to look confident, but if I was asked the time then it was tricky, because not to reply was almost as good as revealing your accent.

I remember once walking across Trafalgar Square and four Leeds fans walked up to me.

'Where are you from, mate?' they asked.

'Surrey,' I replied.

After a few seconds' pause one of them punched me. 'Southern bastard!' he shouted. It had taken him a few seconds to realise where Surrey was. The rule of thumb is that north of Watford is passport country for Cockneys, although it can be just as dangerous going west – or anywhere for that matter.

I remember one cold evening at Eastville, home of Bristol Rovers. Arsenal had just drawn one all and won the tie five–one on aggregate in the League Cup. We walked out of the ground, an old speedway stadium, and across a big open car park. We had about a mile and a half to walk back to our car. No hint of trouble, but I should have realised what sort of area we were in when I saw that the Kentucky Fried Chicken restaurant had metal grilles across the counter. There were two of us, Silly Vince and myself. We walked past a pub that looked rough, outside which stood a large group of young men about twenty-five strong. A big mouth from amongst them confronted someone who was walking along by himself. He'd sussed out a lone Arsenal fan.

'You're not from Bristol are you?'

Quick as a flash, the Arsenal fan put the Bristol big-mouth on the seat of his pants with a corker of a punch, and while his mates were still considering their course of action he had put twenty yards between himself and them. While they were in a state of confusion Vince and I slipped past. We had no scarves on and all the group were busy watching the Arsenal fan sprint up the road, so nobody noticed us. We came to a big roundabout and across the road, leaning up against the railings, was a solitary Rovers fan. He shouted the immortal phrase: 'What's the time, mate?'

I suppose the victory and the unthreatened feeling I had made me forget my brains. Normally one would either try to answer back in a local accent or walk across and punch the person in the face.

'Ten past ten,' I shouted back.

I walked five paces and I heard a shout which set alarm bells ringing in my head: 'Cockneys!'

I looked across the road and saw a group of about eight guys running out of a block of flats. They ran towards us but the speed of the traffic meant that they had to stop at the other side of the road. They seemed in no particular hurry, because we had nowhere to run to. I couldn't seem to think at all; I was trying to, but all I was doing was panicking.

'We're in big trouble, Vince,' I said.

'Come on, bumpkins,' shouted Vince at them.

I don't think Vince was accepting the reality of the situation, and when he turned to me and said, 'Let's run at them to see what they're made of,' I knew I had to think fast. I spotted a pub on our side of the road.

'Let's go for the boozer, Vince, it's our only chance.'

We broke into a quick sprint and darted inside the pub door. This completely threw our pursuers as they expected us to try to make a run for it down the street. I was praying for a back door in the pub to sprint through. We got our breathing space but, alas, no back door, so the only thing to do was backs against the wall and brazen it out. We took up residence at the rear of the pub in the corner of the bar. It was getting near closing time and the landlord was putting all the empty bottles and glasses on the bar counter. 'Ammunition,' I thought.

They came through the door about twenty seconds later and stood at the far end of the bar grinning broadly and laughing. They had got us trapped, knowing we would have to leave at some time; they would get us then. I turned to Vince.

'If they start coming throw glasses, but use the bottles for the close stuff.'

He nodded in agreement.

The landlord, bless him, sensed trouble and phoned the police, who duly turned up and escorted us to our car. As I left the pub I smiled at the guys at the other end of the bar. A very narrow escape.

Half-time at a match: a ten-minute break, the time for people to shuffle out to the area behind the stands or terraces, to queue, often in mud, for stewed tea-leaves mixed with milk in a plastic cup masquerading as a cup of tea and to eat a steak and kidney pie with lumps of gristle big enough to throw at the police. There are the compulsory beefburgers, oozing grease, with a leathery texture and cardboard taste, covered in onions and ketchup. And the push and shove to get into stinking brick and concrete urinals with puddles everywhere. No one ever complained, though, and the way the food was devoured you would have thought it was quite delicious. This was a great time to listen to stories and exchange information and banter. Different groups would stand around acknowledging people with nods or hand-shakes. Some would use the period to parade and pose like peacocks in front of the police and rival fans. The inevitable confrontation of supporters would happen at a fence on one side of the terraces, where opposing fans would swap insults, hurl coins and spit at each other across the meshed divide.

There was even talk about the first forty-five minutes football. If your team was losing, it became imperative that your main rivals' half-time score at another ground was poor in order to lessen the blow, so people were to be seen huddling around anyone with a pocket radio. For many people, the half-time handshaking and back-slapping routine was all part of the fun, and they could often be seen trying to look good just leaning up against a fence.

In the early seventies there didn't seem to be any organisation (sure there were famous names – Johnny Hoy was a known leader at Arsenal); some days everyone went in to take an end, sometimes they didn't. West Ham were the exception, though. In London derbies they always tried to take the opposition's end. In January 1971, in the third round of the FA Cup, we drew Portsmouth away and Arsenal fans in their thousands travelled down there. We simply took over the ground. The Fratton end, home of the Portsmouth fans, was annihilated by the Arsenal mob. There is something about the FA Cup that brings out all the old faces. A day out, loads to drink, seeing people you haven't bumped into for ages. The Cup third round is a must, especially if it's away. Anyone who is anybody turns up. I wouldn't be surprised if Tall Eric doesn't make an appearance one day at an FA Cup tie – minus his white boiler suit, of course!

That year, 1971, we won the League Championship and FA Cup. The final game of the season was at Spurs. Arsenal had to win or draw nil–nil to take the title. There were 50,000 inside and the same number locked out. Again Arsenal fans took over the ground, and our team scored with a few minutes to go. Everyone went berserk. People began to charge on to the pitch. The minutes ticked by and if the referee blew for a foul, then more people charged on. The final whistle went but no one could hear it. Arsenal fans charged. We had won the League on the ground of our fiercest rivals,

Spurs. There were no Spurs fans anywhere, so people started to dig up the turf to take home. Two fans wanted the centre spot and were forced to spin a coin to settle who had it. A story went about that a guy walked into a pub in Islington later that night and put a one-foot-square lump of turf on the bar to use as a beer mat. He slept on the floor in the pub that night and did the same the next day. I wonder how many gardens in north London have a corner which is made up of Tottenham's turf.

Five days after this momentous win Arsenal went to Wembley to play Liverpool in the FA Cup Final. As the triumphant Arsenal march progressed up Wembley Way, every other fan seemed to be sporting a white butcher's coat covered in red, yellow and blue artwork – some good, some awful. Thousands of butchers' shops must have been short of a few coats in the early seventies as the craze for wearing them to matches covered with team colours and motifs really caught on, especially at FA Cup games. The Scousers came down to Wembley in their thousands, but in the car park before the game the Arsenal mob ran the Scousers ragged. The SAB crew from Arsenal also sprayed the subway at Wembley Park station and it adorned the walls for many years afterwards.

I heard a story many years later that during this season Johnny Hoy took a massive firm of guys down to West Ham and more than held his own. They stood their ground on the terraces, chanting 'No surrender' at the oncoming West Ham fans. West Ham always struck fear into me as it did to most Arsenal fans. I have had more people put the frighteners on me down at Upton Park than at any other ground, although I am sure that had I been to some northern grounds more regularly, I would have experienced an even more daunting prospect.

Saturday afternoon at Highbury, through the turnstiles and

up two flights of concrete steps to get to the 'Northbank'. To
enter I had to walk past the green hut bar, precariously sited
and big enough to hold thirty or forty drinkers at a push. I
never passed it in my younger days without hearing the
throaty roar of singing, beer-swilling fans. Once as I walked
past, the sides of the hut were vibrating as the inhabitants
sang 'We're gonna fight, fight, fight for The Arsenal till we
win the Football League' with everything they had got. The
variety of songs that abounded on the terraces in the late sixties and early seventies seemed to epitomise the freshness of
the terrace scene. Fans would take a pop standard then pla-
giarise it with lyrics about their favourite player. Every
player had his own song that fans would sing adoringly, if a
little tunelessly, before, during and after matches. The fans
who originated the songs were anonymous, but a good song
once heard was very quickly adopted by thousands. My
favourite was adapted from 'Mammy' and built around Jon
Sammels: 'I'd walk a million miles for one of your goals, Jon
Sammels.'

The 1972 season came and once more Arsenal took over a
provincial ground in the FA Cup. This time Reading were
the recipients of a mass Cockney invasion. There were no
problems on that day, but later in the season I was to experience real fear and danger.

   British Rail in its infinite wisdom (or more precisely, the
NUR which to us stood for 'No Use Rushing', and if you had
travelled on as many trains as I have you would fully understand the meaning of that) had decided to begin a national
strike on the Monday after Arsenal had drawn one–all in
their semi-final against Stoke City whom we had beaten in
the previous year's semi-final. The replay was set for
Wednesday at Goodison Park, home of Everton FC. This
was 'Scouseland', real indian country. The Liverpool fans
hated Cockneys with a vengeance. I was still at school and

slightly naïve, for I thought that only Arsenal and Spurs fought at football matches. I decided to hitchhike up to Everton and stay with my auntie at Wigan. There was no problem with the hitchhiking, and I arrived on Monday night resplendent in my natty red and white bowler hat, silk scarf and flag.

On the Wednesday I travelled to the ground thinking there would be thousands of Arsenal fans at the match, and I decided to show my colours, so I put on my bowler and unfurled the flag. My scarf was red with cannon motifs on it and was made from silk, which was the fashion then. It was considered macho to tie it around either your wrist or belt; I tied mine around my belt. That was my first error. I marched off down the road feeling quite pleased with myself, a wry smile on my face. Hadn't I beaten British Rail single-handed? In front of me I saw some fans in red and white, about two hundred of them. I walked straight through their midst and as I passed the last couple they turned around and glared at me menacingly. They were Stoke fans, and how I got away with that I will never know.

I decided to head around to the Gwladys Street end. This turned out to be my second mistake, because this was the Everton fans' end. With no large gangs of Arsenal supporters present, someone was bound to pick on lone Arsenal fans; but I was not to know this until later. As I walked along the road a young kid tried to grab my scarf. I spun round and cuffed him across the ear, and he scooted off. I got to the corner of the road and turned left into the street of the main entrance where the players would enter the ground. On the opposite side of the road was a street gang of about twenty Everton fans. They stared hard at me and I knew it spelt trouble, especially when I saw the young kid who had tried to pinch my scarf go up to them and say something. If they were waiting for an easy target then they had found one! Liverpool is a bleak city at the best of times, but whatever colour was around me turned to grey inside my head as fear began to grip me. I was also beginning to feel very lonely. How can you feel lonely with 30,000 people milling around you, going to a football match? Well, I did! I needed help and not a little protection. The Everton fans crossed the street menacingly. I remember one of the faces vividly even to this day. He had a slight mark under his right eye and a smattering of pimples. He was wearing denim and he looked tough and uncompromising. I don't think I could have talked my way out of this one. I started to walk a little faster, but one of them was alongside me.

'Give us your hat, Cockney,' he sneered.

'Piss off, Scouser,' I replied, trying to sound as if I wasn't frightened. He tried to grab it but I moved away and started to walk faster down the road. I broke into a sprint and they all came for me. I saw an opening and ducked into it; it was the main entrance. There would be sanctuary in here, someone to help me at least. I heard a voice behind me. I looked around and saw an elderly gentleman of the type you often see at sports events – unpaid stewards, the sort of people who like to be members of the club and be involved.

'Hey, sonny, what do you think you're doing? You can't stand here, this is for officials only, go and stand out there.'

His arm moved forward to push me out, but I grabbed it and resisted.

'Now listen here,' I said. 'There are twenty guys out there waiting to do me in.'

'Don't be silly, sonny. Come on, let's go and have a look.'

He peered outside but just pretended to have a look around, moving his head from side to side for greater effect. He returned smiling benevolently.

'See, there's no one out there so go on and enjoy the game.' He patted me on the head patronisingly. I suppose I should have stood my ground, but other people in the entrance assured me that it would be okay. I walked out, stuffing my hat into my pocket and trying to make myself inconspicuous. Six feet tall, and with ginger hair – no chance! But what's wrong with trying? I got to the next corner; so far so good, no sign of them. I saw a policeman and thought I would ask for some help.

'Excuse me, officer,' I said. He turned around.

'There is a big gang of Everton fans after me. Could you please walk me to the gate.'

His reply astounded me. 'That will teach you Cockneys to come here. Go on, go and join a gang yourself. Now piss off.'

I stood there dumbfounded, but I thought I might as well just go for it. I walked towards the entrance but twenty yards up the road and blocking my way was the same gang of Everton fans I had encountered earlier. I stood still, thinking 'What shall I do?', but they solved the problem for me. They ran towards me and in what seemed like a split second they were in front of me. One guy arrived first. He flailed through the air with his feet, but he missed. I punched him and caught him in the side of the head. I had one hand on my flag and I swung that at someone else. I thought they might run when they saw I was fighting back. I hit the first one again right on the nose. I felt a kick on the thigh and realised they were all on me. I turned tail and ran as fast as I could, while punches and kicks rained in on me. Fortunately a mounted policeman had seen what had happened and galloped over.

'Stand still, son,' he shouted to me.

The Everton fans scattered everywhere. I could feel a lump on my eye but could not remember anyone striking me. The mounted policeman could see I was shaken up and asked me if I was okay and whether I wanted medical attention. I stammered out my reply.

'No, just walk me to the gate, I'll be okay,' I said. I figured that once I got inside the ground I would be safe.

I walked along with the mounted policeman as escort.

'If you see any of them, point them out,' he said. The truth was that they had been just blurs, except for one. The policeman took me to the turnstiles, and as I got there I threw away the flag; I blamed it for getting me into trouble. I paid my money and went in. Once inside I saw a few Arsenal fans in their mid twenties standing by the bar drinking lager, so I put my hat back on. I told them what had happened and they said 'Stick with us, son, we'll look after you.'

Great, I thought, safe at last, but just before kick-off I lost them – or perhaps they thought I would burden them and lost me. I was on my own again. I went on to the terraces and decided to stand on my own near the front. No one bothered me during the game, but I didn't feel easy. The match went well, Arsenal winning two–one after being one–nil down. At the end I went to run on to the pitch to congratulate the Arsenal players, but as I went forward an Everton fan grabbed my hat and turned to run off. I caught hold of him, turned and clipped him around the side of the head.

'Let go or I'll hit you hard,' I said.

Before I knew what was going on I was set upon by about half a dozen guys. I didn't hang around. I was down on my hands and knees belting up the terraces, going through people's legs with these guys trying to kick me. All I could hear was people saying 'Steady on' or 'What do you think you're doing?' Nobody tried to help. I got to the exit. The guys had given up trying to kick me after about five terrace steps, but as far as I knew they were right behind me. I made my way up the road at some speed to where my uncle was going to meet me to take me back to Wigan. All I had left was my silk scarf tied around my belt, and I untied it and stuffed it in my pocket. I was very frightened and was really glad to see my uncle. He asked me how I had got on.

'Okay,' I said.

'What's that mark on your face?' he asked.

'Nothing, it's where I hit my face on the banner in the excitement.'

'You should be more careful,' he said.

We got into the car, and to add insult to injury I saw the guys who had stolen my hat walking through the traffic, looking extremely pleased with themselves.

The season of 1972 ended with Arsenal's defeat in the FA Cup Final by Leeds, but I kept out of any trouble that day and travelled to and from Wembley with my dad. That summer I left school and started work in a butcher's shop, which necessitated working Saturday mornings, so away games were relegated to special occasions, London derbies and FA Cup ties. I still went to every Arsenal home match; but now the terrace fun was to be found with my local team.

2

Leatherhead

Leatherhead is a sleepy Surrey town with a football team nicknamed 'The Tanners'. Their ground was a simple affair alongside the River Mole. One end was a grassy bank, one side and the other end just flat grass-covered ground. At the other side were two corrugated-iron stands covering a small amount of terracing at each end of the pitch. In the middle of these there was a small number of seats which backed on to the clubhouse where many Saturday nights of my youth were spent at the football club discos. The iron stand at the far end of the pitch as you entered the ground became known affectionately as 'The Shed'. However, the real memory of Leatherhead, for most people, is of rainy days, for then the entire pitch becomes mud.

My first experience of Leatherhead was when I was ten years old and they drew Hendon in the FA Amateur Cup. The game really captured the imagination of the whole town. It was the quarter-final and everyone wanted to be there. Local traders sold tickets. The ground, crammed with over 4,000 people, was a sight to behold. Everywhere was covered in green and white. There was a guy with a huge drum strapped to his chest and he was marching around the pitch banging it, chanting 'Tanners, Tanners'. All the young kids who were sitting by the side of the pitch jumped in behind him, myself included. The crowd cheered and we all marched around waving our scarves. The Leatherhead players came out and everyone went berserk; people were running all over the pitch. The police (I think there were about four of them), along with club officials, were trying to get the crowd back beyond the touchlines. 'Ee eye adio we're gonna win the cup,' chanted the crowd; but reality prevailed. Hendon, who were one of the top amateur teams of the day, trounced Leatherhead three–nil.

I did my bit to help the team, though. I spent the first half lobbing chunks of wet mud at John Swannell's head (he was the Hendon goalkeeper). I remember hitting him with a juicy dollop and he turned around, his face full of rage, and all the other young urchins shouted out 'Great shot, Ginger!' But our fun was not to last. A burly sergeant was placed behind the goal and he threatened us with dire consequences if we threw any more mud. Leatherhead fans went home afterwards deflated but convinced they would one day taste glory. In fact, Leatherhead would taste success against professional teams, but never again would the ground see a crowd as big as that or the town experience such Cup fever.

The years passed by and Leatherhead became an enjoyable place to be on Saturdays, mostly in the evenings for the disco. The Amateur Cup was fun. Leatherhead always lost, of course, but in 1971 we did at last have a team. We drew Blyth Spartans out of the hat, the North East's finest. Leatherhead drew nil–nil up there. I didn't travel up to Blyth but I heard all the stories down at the local youth centre all week. The consensus was that the Geordies were mental. Yogi Hughes had told us they had been chased all over the fields as soon as they got off the coaches. Amongst football fans it is dishonourable to run. The Millwall fans' proudest boast is 'Millwall never run', but I am sure that everyone has run at some time. We were determined that anyone who came down to Leatherhead would be made to suffer for the hiding they had given us at Blyth.

Martin Collins, who is a well-known personality around Leatherhead and is now a pillar of society, was at that time a bit of a thug. He had been arrested along with Steve Chitty and a few others for fighting – a sort of Custer's Last Stand, but his glib tongue had got them off. He had got up a little firm ready to inflict damage upon these invading foreigners. It was common knowledge that they didn't speak the same language as us. We were loyal, fierce and passionate and we also had the 'Shed' to defend. Nobody could take the Shed. These northern heathens wouldn't dare, would they?

I got to the ground about two o'clock, and bumped into Trevor Gorrard, who told me excitedly: 'There are Blyth fans everywhere but a few of them have already had a kicking up the town.'

The trouble was that we were just fifteen, with boots bigger than our muscles. The Blyth fans all seemed in their late teens or early twenties and they were all drinking. I was dumbfounded; they didn't seem nervous at all. We all walked around to the Shed. They wouldn't dare come in the Shed, I told myself. We walked around there and all the Leatherhead fans were packed in. At least sanity was restored here. Everyone was singing 'Leatherhead for the Cup'. Today was definitely going to be our day. As I was chattering away I saw two Geordies who had obviously had a lot to drink walk out across the pitch, which as usual had plenty of mud on it. They had a flag with them and Blyth scarves in their hands. When they got to the middle they put down the two scarves across the centre spot to form a cross and stuck the flag in the ground. It was tantamount to a conquering army raising the standard. They then got on their hands and knees and started praying and milking the cheers of the Blyth fans. Of course, we were all booing like mad. To our astonishment they walked back to the Blyth fans and left the flag and scarves in the middle of the pitch. This was a symbol of domination. We couldn't stand for this. Trevor Gorrard turned around to me and said, 'Come on Ginger, let's go and nick them.'

I thought 'What a good idea' but was wary about getting caught by the two guys, who were much older than me. Still, what the hell. Four of us ran out on to the pitch: Keith Chitty, Phil Stevenson, Trevor and myself. Although Phil was only fifteen he had grown a moustache, had tattoos and had also received a school suspension. He lived in the local children's home and was a distinctly tough individual who wasn't bothered about getting a punch in the mouth. Keith would do anything for a laugh as long as his mum didn't find out – because Keith, like all football fans, was frightened of mum. Trevor was just loud. He was always going to thump someone but never did; one meets plenty of Trevor types at football matches.

I was immediately struck by how muddy the pitch was. I could hardly keep my feet. We ran out to the centre to the cheers of the Shed ringing in our ears. I snapped the flag in half, and we stamped on the scarves then held them aloft like Indians holding up scalps. All four of us were laughing aloud! What a giggle! We showed the Geordies. I didn't even hear the growling and swearing coming from the Blyth fans' section, but the next thing I knew there were four gorillas coming across the pitch at us. I don't think a discussion of football was on their minds. Trevor was already heading back to the Shed, and it was every man for himself.

'Grab the scarves!' shouted Trevor.

Keith and I snatched them up and we headed off towards the goal. I suddenly realised that these Geordie loonies wanted Keith and me. I tried to speed up but the faster I tried to run, the slower I seemed to be going. I turned around and one of them seemed to have gained twenty yards in ten paces. I dropped the scarf I was holding and so did Keith, and we headed away towards the sanctuary of the Shed. They reached the scarves, picked them up, gave a 'V' sign and turned away. We were feted like returning war heroes.

'What was it like, Ginger?'

'Yeah, it was easy,' I said. But the truth was that my heart was beating at a hundred miles per hour and I was petrified. In order to go to the toilet I still had to walk past the stand they were in. I was saved that problem by everyone peeing against the wall behind the Shed terrace at half-time. Just before kick-off Martin Collins and his firm walked across the pitch past the Geordies, who shouted a few obscenities and Martin and his crew returned the compliment. Unfortunately John Weller, who was barely fifteen but fancied his chances as a hard nut, decided that a fight was necessary, and while everyone was still laughing about our exploits and taking no notice of the Geordies, four of them jumped over the barrier and proceeded to kick John into next week. We all surged on to the pitch and got a few good punches in, but the police intervened. They shepherded everyone back to their stands while the Geordies had a good laugh. The truth of the matter was that they were too good for us: we were barely old enough to shave, they were probably veterans of dozens of terrace fights.

The game itself was predictable. Leatherhead were the better team but Blyth won one–nil from a breakaway goal. After the game we spilled out of the ground and Goody, a local halfwit, put a stone through the Blyth players' coach window. We acted as if we would tear any Geordie limb from limb, but hoped not to find any because we didn't think we could win a fight. Terrace fighting at football grounds is all about winning; only nutters don't care if they get a kick-ing. We surged across the River Mole bridge. I was about ten paces behind Trevor Gorrard. A car window was wound down and a broad Geordie accent shouted out: 'Go on, lads, smash up the town.'

That was all Trevor needed. He ran up and kicked hell out of the car door.

'Get out, you pigs. Come on, let's turn the car over,' he screamed. Unfortunately, nobody told the Geordies they were supposed to be frightened and sit there and take it. Out they jumped, and one of them grabbed hold of me. I stood there thinking my next destination was the river.

'Who's your friend?' he asked.

'I don't know, he comes from miles away. First time I've seen him,' I stammered. The driver shouted to his mate, who had hold of me, to let go.

'Come on, Jimmy, let's drive up the road and see if we can catch the bugger who kicked the car.'

Jimmy let go and got back into the car, which sped off. Trevor was long gone and I saw him about ten minutes later in Woolworths. His face was flushed. He had been running. The car had pulled into the car park of the Prince of Wales public house, they had spotted him and chased him.

'Hello, Trevor, you okay?' I asked.

'Yeah, Ginger, I'm going back to kick the other car door when it gets dark. I am going to give them a matching pair. Those Geordie bastards are having a drink in the Prince of Wales.'

It was all bravado. He wouldn't go within half a mile of that car. We all ambled up the road leaving the Geordies to head back north. We were left with our Saturday night disco at Leatherhead Football Club, of course, where we told the girls outrageous stories of heroism and spectacular fights. I was the hero of the hour, the guy who had stood up to the Geordies. I strutted around like a peacock all night, even taking a girl out to the centre spot to show her where I had defied an army of Blyth fans and upheld the honour of Leatherhead. She thought I was smashing.

There wasn't to be another day like Blyth until a few seasons later. Leatherhead had finally got a strong team together. We had reached the semi-finals of the FA Amateur Cup in which we were due to play Ilford. We had a brilliant centre-forward, Nobby Skinner, who was mustard. Nobby could run any defence ragged. Unfortunately, the venue chosen for the match was Millwall FC. Millwall: the word sent shivers down my spine; the hardest fans in the land. They had once taken the Everton end in an FA Cup-tie. Everyone knows dockers are tough. We were scared, but we had our stories. One guy came down to the disco and said that Millwall would be supporting Leatherhead because we were south of the River Thames while Ilford was north of the river and near West Ham, who were hated by Millwall. Anyway, we would go along and hope for the best. Besides, Millwall were away to Cardiff so any Millwall fan worth his salt would be down there – or at least that's what we hoped.

The talking was over and match day arrived. Fear was definitely not on for Leatherhead fans. Andy Montague (known as Monty), Mark Butcher and I set off for the match in Andy Wickens' motor. It was a grey box-shaped Renault, one of the ugliest cars ever made. We didn't care. It would be cheap and safer than going by train. Off we chugged down the Old Kent Road talking about all the people who had presented excuses for their non-attendance at the match, only wishing that we had had a wedding to go to or a new girlfriend's parents to meet. We laughed aloud, calling so-and-so a tosser for losing his nerve. But the laughter stopped abruptly when we came to the rows of dingy terraced houses, boarded-up shops and litter-strewn streets. It looked rough and we were definitely entering a different world. Andy said 'Shall we stop for a drink?' but Mark, who was only sixteen and looked even younger, didn't think he would get served. I was not keen to go into a pub, despite my bravado about how I was going to fight all and sundry. We drove down a road with houses boarded up and Andy was reluctant to park his car in it; but we could see the floodlight pylons. 'Park it up, Andy, who's going to nick this rust bucket?' said Monty.

'It's getting the tyres slashed I'm worried about,' replied Andy.

We had a discussion and finally agreed to leave the car in this road. When we got out of the car Andy put on his Leatherhead scarf and I led the way as usual. We were all nervous, ready to run at any moment. We turned the corner and saw the ground. It was very unglamorous, not like Highbury or Tottenham. It was the ground of a club that had spent all its life in the lower reaches of the Football League. But the fans were in the first division of the fighting league table and that was what was on our minds. We came to the entrance; not a Millwall fan in sight. Green and white everywhere. I spotted Bob Baker. Bob is like a loud Desperate Dan. He also has a tooth missing in the front, so when he smiles he looks funny. He shouted at me.

'See Millwall have shit down from us.'

Perhaps he was right. We entered the ground and went into the Cold Blow Lane end – the home end of the notorious Millwall fans. Three sides of the ground were covered terraces and at the opposite end behind the goal was New Cross dog-racing stadium, a relic from the days when the docklands had a working population. At about 2.45 I heard more chanting. More Leatherhead fans. We were everywhere; we sang and danced. We had taken the Millwall end. There were a few Millwall fans in there, but not enough to bother us. Out came the teams. Ilford had about two coachloads of mums and dads. We were there in strength, every man a fighter (or so we all thought).

All the older guys, the ones we looked up to, went and stood at the bar on the terraces by the halfway line. Apart from the seated area you could walk around the ground at Millwall on that day. We were dominating the place. We would win the game and return to Leatherhead with fantastic stories. This was fun. But no one told us that the pubs chucked out at about 3.10. By 3.20 a small group of Millwall fans had turned up, by half-time a few more – I suppose about fifty of them. They wanted sport. They jeered at our songs and made derogatory remarks. I had seen enough.

'Come on, Monty, let's go and stand at the bar and get some alcohol inside us, so when we get hit it won't hurt as much.'

We trundled off to the bar and started drinking. There was an added bonus of the protection of some of the older guys. I even started watching the game, distancing myself from what was bound to happen on the terraces. Half-time came. Now at that time the practice during amateur games was to stand behind the goal your team was defending. This could be where the saying 'Get right behind your team' comes from. The regular Leatherhead fans all trundled out of the Cold Blow Lane end to support Leatherhead, who would now be attacking that end in the second half. Kevin Biggs and two of his friends decided to take the shortest possible route to the other end, across the pitch. They ran with a Leatherhead flag raised above their heads. The Millwall fans went crazy.

'Get off our pitch!' they screamed.

So far they had been indifferent towards us, but the novelty had worn off. We had left the Cold Blow Lane end and we weren't going to return. A few Leatherhead fans left at that end were told to leave. Andy Wickens was sitting on the terraces when he felt a kick in the back.

'Shift, fatso.'

He looked up at a Millwall fan who was dressed in a white

rollneck sweater which was tucked inside his jeans at the waist. Andy stood up; he wouldn't need to be told twice. I was standing at the bar on the halfway line when Keith Chitty, Phil Stevenson, Dave Cromie and Nigel Wood walked past. Woody was a local nutcase whose favourite Saturday night hobby was disco brawling. Football matches acted like a magnet to his type, drawing them on to the terraces. Woody had jet-black hair and eyes that were definitely too close together for comfort. Dave was a nice guy, but his friendship with Woody meant he had to get involved in a few fights.

'Where you going, Keith?' I asked.

'Up the Cold Blow to have a go at the Millwall.'

Monty and I looked at each other incredulously. 'Fight Millwall? More drinks, barmaid, and make them large ones!!'

'You coming, Ginger?'

'No, I think I'll pass on this one.'

I don't even drink shorts, but I had to raise my pain threshold in case I was needed. They got to the end of the alleyway which connects the side terrace to the walkway which goes behind the Cold Blow Lane end. At the end of the alleyway were three Millwall fans just looking and wait-ing with expectant expressions – not the sort of expression you would see on a commuter waiting for a train, but the type you only see on a football fan waiting for a fight. But who will make the first move?

'Come on lads, let's get them,' shouted Woody.

He ran down the alley towards them. Keith, Phil and Dave just stood there. Woody got within range of the three Millwall fans. One punch, and Woody hit the concrete with a thud. The three of them set about him with their boots, but I think he was out cold. After about twenty seconds they ran towards Keith, Phil and Dave, who ran. I don't blame them – I would have done the same. The Millwall fans got halfway up the alley and stopped, shrugged and turned. They were laughing. This was fun!! They ambled back down the alley and just for good measure they gave Woody another kicking. This was a 'friendly' kicking, just to let him know he had met Millwall. They then strolled off nonchalantly. Dave walked down to where Woody was lying, picked him up and brought him over to the bar area. Woody was in a terrible mess and his face had lumps coming up all over it. He was semi-conscious and didn't realise he had been sick down the front of his coat. I felt ill just looking at him, but was secretly glad it was him and not me. Phil Stevenson was busy trying to get a team to go down the Cold Blow Lane end to do the Millwall. No one wanted to be seen to be scared, so we all said, 'Yes, let's go.' Everyone was petrified, though. I had no intention of going down there. Bob Baker came up to me.

'Come on, Ginger, let's go.'

'You're joking, Bob, I'm not going down there to run back here.'

'You shitout, Ginger. I'm going to tell everyone you're a coward.'

'All right, Bob.'

I turned to Monty. 'Drink up, Monty, let's go.'

We walked down the alleyway but with no conviction in our step. We encountered no Millwall fans but they could see us coming. The back of the Cold Blow Lane was upon us and we massed at the bottom of the steps that led on to the terraces, waiting for someone to lead us into battle. I went and stood on the steps about six steps up. A Millwall fan walked down towards the hot-dog van which we were standing around, coming down the steps towards the sixty-strong Leatherhead army. He was a big guy. 'Shall I belt him?' I thought. He walked past me and straight up to the van to buy two hot-dogs. 'I'll get him on the way back,' I thought. 'As he walks up the steps I shall hit him and knock him down.'

He turned and walked back up the steps. My heart was thumping, for I was going to belt this guy, and he looked even bigger coming up the steps He glanced at the Leatherhead fans, who were discussing their assault tactics. He was laughing. As he got alongside me he looked at me as if to say, 'Don't try it.' I lost my nerve. I thought he might have been a little frightened, but in fact it was us, the quivering army, who were scared. Phil Stevenson led the Leatherhead fans up the steps and into the Cold Blow Lane end. Millwall's ground is called 'The Den', and their nickname is 'The Lions'. This really was a case of the Christians going to the slaughter in the Lions' den. I took up the rear in case the Millwall fans came out of the other exit, but basically I was running scared. As the bulk of the Leatherhead fans went into the Cold Blow Lane, I turned away and the next thing I knew I was bundled in the back. I hit the stair rail with a crash. I turned around and all I could see were frightened faces charging back down the steps.

'The Millwall are coming,' shouted a voice.

That was all I needed; I was off down the steps. I thought I was a fast runner, but people were coming past me with ease. Ginger Penny came past me, his legs going as high as his head. Just in front of me he tripped and crashed down the steps, ending up at the bottom. He lay there moaning. I got to the bottom of the steps and realised that the Millwall weren't even chasing us.

'Stop running,' I shouted.

Phil Stevenson came down the steps, shouting, 'You wankers, we had them on the run.'

We held a council of war again at the bottom of the steps, but the general consensus was that we had acquitted ourselves quite well so we would retire while we were even. We ambled off to the other end and Ginger Penny limped off with his mates. I was standing up against the rail near the bar on the halfway line with Dave Cromie and Woody. The three Millwall fans who had earlier given Woody a hiding came over. One pulled out a carving knife.

'You lot are going to get some of this later.'

All the time he had a sickly smile on his face. (Years later I was to see this smile again.) They looked at Woody. 'He's had enough,' said Dave.

'Had enough, he ain't had half enough and neither have all of you,' one of them sneered.

I had certainly had enough. I went and got Monty, Andy and Mark. It was about ten minutes from the final whistle, and we got ready to shoot away. When it blew we shot out of the exit towards our car. Every street looked the same: bleak and uncompromising. At every alleyway we passed we were fearful that Millwall fans who knew the area would emerge. We got back to the car, jumped in, and Andy drove off at high speed. I felt safe at last. I didn't care about the others. Ginger Penny had broken his ankle and had been taken to hospital, but I hadn't given him a second thought. As we sped away from Millwall it suddenly dawned on us that Leatherhead had lost one–nil. But the game was a blur. Many years later I heard that Nobby Skinner had been drunk the night before and had played a stinker. At the time I didn't even know if he had played at all.

I have never met anybody from that day who actually ran from Millwall. The saying goes that you must learn to walk before you can run, but on the terraces it is the exact opposite. Running is an absolute essential, although admitting that fact is a heinous sin and anyone who does so usually adds that they ran only because everybody else did and, of course, that they were the last to run. Some people never run – or so they say. I have seen idiots who stand and try to fight twenty or thirty advancing fans, although I'm sure they didn't make a habit of it! In any football crowd there are compulsive runners, people who at one sight of the opposing group will be up on their toes, like a twitching gazelle who has just smelt a cheetah, ready to run as soon as the group begins to charge. The same people would also charge after opposing fans like crazed animals if they saw them running in fear. It is to be hoped that there will be in the group people who will stand whatever the odds, and everybody looks to these people to hold the group together. If they show fear or hesitation, panic will set in. Then again you have the famous 'Stand and Fight!' crier. He will 'stand' usually in the centre or rear, although if nobody takes any notice of him then he can run with impunity and tell everyone he tried his best. Of course, if his cry saves the day then he becomes a hero.

Some groups of fans acquired reputations for not running, and Millwall were supposedly top of the list. The worst feeling when you are fleeing is seeing people come past you and sensing that the pursuing mob will catch you. Most people when forced to run, though, find all the speed they require. While running all loyalty to friends and comrades is forgotten; it's every man for himself.

The conversation before some matches was often all about which fans had run from which others, and there was huge excitement in making groups of rival fans run from you. Often hundreds would run after only three or four punches had been thrown. In such a case, the person who had led the group and thrown the punches enjoyed a real feeling of power and a sort of kudos amongst the other fans.

The Amateur Cup was always to elude Leatherhead. It was later replaced by the FA Vase and FA Trophy, because the Football Association deemed there was no such thing as an amateur footballer.

The FA Cup is open to all senior clubs in the Football Association and although most people only see the final in May on the television, the competition starts in August every season when the small fry begin the process which every club hopes will lead to a big-money match against a professional club. It was the season of 1974–75. Leatherhead had got through four qualifying rounds and had won their first-round proper match two–nil against Bishop's Stortford (another semi-professional team). In the second round, Colchester (a professional team) came out of the hat. Colchester were famous for beating the mighty Leeds United in 1971. Now it was their turn to face a little team. The pubs were buzzing because Leatherhead really did have a good football team. They also had Chris Kelly, a talented extrovert both on and off the field.

We got to the ground and started talking to a few people. The Colchester fans had arrived at about two o'clock and taken our place in the Shed. But thirty minutes later Leatherhead had stormed in and there was a huge punch-up, as a result of which the Shed had been re-taken. The Colchester fans had then taken up residence predominantly in the other stand, but there were supporters all around the ground from Colchester. We went into the Shed, but it was too crowded. A Colchester fan who really thought he was Jack the Lad walked in front of the Shed and gesticulated with his hand that he thought we were wankers. He walked around the corner and Eric Phillips punched him right on the side of the head. He hit the mud and in went the boot. Today was not going to be another Blyth. Eric was a nutcase, and tough with it. He had just come out of borstal. He was tall, wiry, covered in tattoos and had spent his time in borstal training with weights every day.

There was a large contingent of police at the match and they moved into the Shed, arresting a few Leatherhead fans. One policeman came upon the Colchester fan lying in the mud and phoned for an ambulance. I went and stood behind the goal. It was very muddy. Yogi Hughes, Monty and Keith came and joined me. Leatherhead got a free kick and scored a brilliant goal: one–nil. We went crazy. The Colchester fans were not amused. Ten guys spotted us behind the goal and decided to come round. They walked past us, eyeing us up. We pretended to ignore them but kept one eye on the game and the other on them. I was standing slightly away from the rest and one Colchester fan came and stood next to me.

'Go on, Billy,' someone shouted.

I had Billy standing on my left and the other nine on my right. Billy was obviously going to start a fight. Next thing I felt a kick on my right leg. I looked around and saw the Colchester fans coming at me. I swung round and punched Billy right on the jaw. He was quite big, but he went straight down into the mud. Monty immediately kicked him in the ribs and Keith gave him one in the back for good measure. Billy was down. I turned to the other Colchester fans. They had just seen their main man dismantled. I went at them throwing punches wildly, but they had seen enough. Off they went. I kicked a couple up the backside. A policeman came up to me.

'He started it,' I said.

Everyone backed me up. The policeman helped Billy, who was covered in mud, to his feet, and sent him on his way, telling me to watch my behaviour. Billy walked past me.

'Bye-bye, Billy.'

'I can recommend a good dry cleaner,' shouted Monty. We were all laughing.

Half-time arrived and we all massed in the car park, but the police prevented us from getting to the Colchester fans. We were rampant now, and the Colchester supporters were wary. After the game we strolled up the road. We had won one–nil. The Colchester fans had police protection, so why bother to get arrested? However, Billy and his little firm had not forgotten me. I told everyone I would see them later, and walked off. I got to the park, turned around and there was Billy and his mob right behind me.

'You ginger bastard,' shouted one.

Off I sprinted, with them in hot pursuit. They chased me for about half a mile but I ducked into a road and was gone. I headed back into town and met up with everyone else telling them of my lucky escape. Who cares? We are into the hat on Monday morning.

The FA Cup draw is a peculiar British institution. It is a radio event which could never make the transition to television. It happens at 12.30 p.m. on the Monday after the previous round games on the Saturday. A radio sports commentator announces in a hushed voice to heighten the tension: 'I have just had the signal that the draw for the next round of the Football Association Challenge Cup is about to begin.'

The participating clubs are represented as numbered wooden balls which are placed in a cotton bag (the hat). Just before the draw is started the bag of balls is rattled next to the microphone, to prove, I presume, that everything is above board and numbers will be drawn at random. Football fans all over the country in shops, factories and schools huddle around the radio waiting for their team's name to be read out. Stern-voiced gentlemen call out the numbers and announce the teams in ever-so-correct English and with no emotion in their voices. At the other end of the radio sets, however, it's often bedlam as fans rejoice when a plum draw comes out of the hat.

It was the FA Cup third round. Enter the giants – Arsenal, Spurs, Manchester United. They are in the hat on level terms with Leatherhead. The draw begins and team after team comes out. A number is called. 'Brighton.' A pause. The next number is called. 'Will play Leatherhead.'

When your team comes out of the hat the rest of the draw becomes irrelevant. Brighton away. There was no doubt we would go out of the Cup. After all, they were in the Third

Division. But what a day out this was going to be. The young guys, myself included, were planning a monster party. Everybody who was worth their salt would be there defending Leatherhead's honour. Coaches were being organised, and Monty, Yogi Hughes, Jeff Stracey and myself were booked up to travel with Leatherhead Supporters Club. The coach was leaving at eleven o'clock. Jeff turned up. He was just nineteen but had spent most of the previous four years in one borstal or another. He told outrageous stories which made us laugh, but he seemed to attract punch-ups wherever he went. We knew we were in for a lively day out.

Once in Brighton we all piled into The Seagull, a pub near the ground. The locals were surprised to see so many Leatherhead fans, and when we got inside there were already thirty or forty other Leatherhead fans in there. The Brighton fans thought it was funny the way we talked of victory. After all, they were bound to win so they saw us as no threat. We sat around in the pub drinking heartily. Every time another Leatherhead fan came through the door he was greeted like a long-lost relative. There was much back-slapping, shaking hands and telling each other who had arrived and who was where.

Someone came into the pub with some hot news. 'I have just come past the pub up the road and there is a tidy firm of Brighton in there.' Everybody gathers round asking the same silly questions: 'Are they rough-looking?', 'How many of them?' etc.

Two-thirty approached; thirty minutes to kick-off. People began to drink up and leave. Our little group left about five minutes later to make the short walk down to the ground. We walked past the home supporters' end. There were groups of Brighton fans milling around; this could be a flash-point area. They looked at us but we took no notice, just walked around to the other end. The opposing supporters' end was in a dead-end street so the only way out was past the Brighton end, but I didn't see it as a problem because we'd be lucky to lose three–nil so the home fans wouldn't bother us.

We entered the ground and made our way to the buffet bar in the left-hand corner. All the Leatherhead fans were in there. The same ritual that we had gone through in The Seagull happened again. In the corner of the bar looking on disdainfully was a large group of Brighton fans. We chanted 'Leatherhead!' They shouted 'Tossers!' They were aggressive and rude. We couldn't frighten them – or could we? Biggsy had a great idea. He started chanting 'Millwall!' That's it! What a great idea! They might not be frightened of Leatherhead, but Millwall would put the fear of God into them. After the third chant of 'Millwall' I noticed the Brighton fans were laughing their heads off. We had failed to frighten them.

We made our way on to the terrace and I took up my position directly behind the goal. A large group of Brighton fans was herded down the front by the police and escorted to the opposite end. We cheered loudly, and chanted mockingly at them. We kidded ourselves that they had left because the Leatherhead mob had put the frighteners on them. This still left a group of about forty Brighton fans who took up a position directly behind the goal just in front of us.

Someone tapped me on the back. I turned around and Silly Vince was standing there. Despite his stupid act he was really quite intelligent and could spot trouble on the terraces. In addition, he never ran if his mate was in trouble: the sort of person you need on the terraces. He was standing there with his right arm in plaster. He had fallen over after he had come out of the local pub a couple of weeks earlier.

Leatherhead came out and we cheered like mad. We made every second count, because this would be our day in the spotlight. The first half went well, with Leatherhead holding their own on the pitch. Jeff Stracey caused an incident when he started singing his favourite song, 'Harry Roberts is our friend, he kills coppers'.* A policeman moved forward to grab hold of him and Jeff belted him. More police moved in and despite Jeff continuing to throw punches they manhandled him out of the ground. When they got him outside the sergeant said to his PCs, 'Hold on to the prat,' and while they held on to Jeff the sergeant walloped him once in the stomach then backhanded him across the face. Jeff was lying on the pavement doubled up in agony. The sergeant addressed him sternly like a teacher admonishing a little boy.

'This is how we deal with football idiots like you down here. Now piss off and if I see you again you're nicked.'

Monty, who had followed Jeff out of the ground, helped him to his feet and walked up the road with him. They waited outside until the second half when the exit gates would open. Monty never saw Leatherhead's goal, but he did see Jeff try to help a Leatherhead fan escape arrest then have the dubious privilege of standing next to Jeff at the Brighton end. As soon as the exit gates were opened Jeff charged in and tried to start a fight by singing 'Leatherhead!' That was Jeff for you. Poor old Monty was a nervous wreck by the end of the day. The game was going well; Kelly got the ball, started running and kept going. He shot, the ball hit the post, GOAL! I don't believe it, it's there. We erupted with joy, but immediately the Brighton fans in front of us went berserk. They surged up the terraces punching and kicking any Leatherhead fans in their path. I saw a Leatherhead fan go down and the boot go in. I pushed forward with flying fists and feet and forced them back. Silly Vince was alongside me whacking all and sundry on the head with his plaster cast. A big gap appeared with Vince, myself and a few other Leatherhead supporters on one side. Ten feet away stood

*Harry Roberts was jailed for life for the murder of an Essex policeman.

the snarling group of Brighton fans; a temporary stand-off. They sneered at us and beckoned us forward.

'What's the score, seaweed face?' I jeered. This incensed them, causing them to charge up the terraces intent on causing me bodily harm. There was a brief flurry of punches but by this time more Leatherhead fans had moved forward and we easily pushed them back. We were standing behind a barrier and as the Brighton fans were about to charge again a couple of police moved in and dragged a couple of them away. A few more police stood in the gap that had appeared and I went and stood in it as well to laugh at the remaining Brighton fans. One of them went mad at my laughing face and charged forward to thump me, but only succeeded in getting himself arrested. As he was marched past me he aimed a kick at my leg.

'Say goodbye to fifty pounds, limp-brain,' was my retort.

A Brighton fan walked forward and spoke to me.

'That was our pal who got nicked and we're going to get you for it after the game, because you stick out like a sore thumb.'

'Don't worry about me, mate, I don't frighten easily. Now run along before I'm tempted to give you a slap,' I replied.

I looked around to survey who would back me up. Jeff and Monty were gone. Silly Vince had broken his plaster cast and was complaining about the pain in his arm. Despite my brash exterior I was worried. I would have to hang around for the coach pick-up. With about five minutes of the match remaining I was feeling very nervous about my survival chances, so I decided to slip away to the back of the stand ready to make a quick getaway at the final whistle. I hoped the Brighton fans had forgotten about me, but as I glanced around I realised they still had me in their sights.

The final whistle went, and while all the other Leatherhead fans cheered a great victory I shot out of the exit and sprinted up the road. Behind the Brighton end was a small park and amongst the milling people and falling darkness I lost my pursuers. Dom Kirby and his younger brother, along with Rus Whiffen and Steve Mappin, spotted me.

'What's the matter, Ginger? You look worried.'

'I'd take those scarves off if I were you. There's a group of about twenty or so Brighton fans gunning for me, but any Leatherhead fans will suffice. I'm lying low while the heat dies down!'

They walked away, laughing at my imaginary fears, but as they walked around the corner they were set upon by a group of Brighton fans. Steve Mappin lost four front teeth to a steel toe-capped boot. When I returned to our coach pick-up point half an hour later I burst out laughing at the state of them. It was the first time I had met Steve and he was not amused by my laughter.

'What the hell do you think you're laughing at, you bastard, look at the state of us,' he shouted. This made me laugh even more.

I slapped Steve on the back. 'Cheers, mate, you got the beating earmarked for me.'

Steve was to become a great friend of mine, for unbeknown to me he was also a big Arsenal fan.

Five-thirty approached and we all stood outside the ground waiting for our coaches. A small group of police guarded us. We chattered jubilantly among ourselves. Jeff was telling his stories, still unable to believe how he had avoided arrest. Monty swore to me that he would never attend another football match with Jeff as long as he lived, and he has stayed true to his word. Keith Oram, who was Leatherhead's biggest fan and was destined to become team manager one day, had a radio. He switched it on.

'Gather round lads, it's the Cup draw.'

'That's not till Monday.'

'Wrong again, Ginger, they've put it forward to Saturday night for the pools' companies.'

We huddled around the pocket radio. It crackled as the numbers were called out. We were all hoping for Arsenal, Chelsea, Spurs or Manchester United.

'Leatherhead,' the name is called, a roar goes up, 'will play Leicester City.'

Whoops of delight. A First Division team at home. The season was turning into a fairy tale. How would it end?

A board meeting was held during the week and the tie was switched to Leicester's ground, Filbert Street. Leatherhead was to get a share of a 30,000 gate, whereas a home tie would have meant 10,000 people being turned away. It didn't bother the fans one bit. The talk in the pubs was about just one thing. Who are you going with? How are you getting to Leicester? The tabloid press seized upon Leatherhead and started running stories. Chris Kelly revelled in the attention and started giving interviews saying how he would rip Leicester to pieces. The *Daily Mail* nicknamed Kelly the 'Leatherhead Lip', and the name stuck. Despite the fact that the Leicester team contained full England international players, Chris Kelly was adamant that Leatherhead would do it. Whatever happened, Leatherhead was at last on the map.

I decided to travel up to Leicester in Jack Legg's car. I presumed that Eric Phillips and Stewart Francis would be with him. Leggy is big and fat. He is also one of the funniest people I have ever met in my life. When Leggy and Stewart get together in a pub it is as good as Morecambe and Wise. We decided to leave at seven o'clock in the morning. Imagine my horror when they picked me up and I saw that sitting in the front seat of the car, instead of Eric, was Leggy's girlfriend, Jenny. What sort of day out were we going to have? I wondered. We got to Leicester at about 9.30 and went into the town centre. Jenny wanted to look around the shops. Eric, I discovered, had gone by train with the other Bookham idiots when he found out that Jenny was to come along. Jenny had insisted that Leggy take her, because her best friend had been taken to Brighton and had enjoyed her day out. I had the right hump and sat through the whole journey planning my escape while thinking wistfully about the great time being had by all on the train. I had to get away from them, but I also needed to get home after the game. It got to 10.30 and I suggested we all go for a drink. Jenny did not think that too good an idea as we might get drunk; I thought that was the general idea. Then I had a brainwave.

'Why don't we go and park the car in a good position near the ground, then we won't have to worry about it. We can nip down to the ground and buy some seats.'

Jenny thought this a splendid idea.

Leggy parked the car and as we got out I said I needed to nip into a shop on the corner. 'I'll catch you up in a minute.'

'OK, Ginger, see you down the ticket office.'

I was off. Enjoy yourself, I thought. I found a pub that had just opened, the Market Inn. I went in and sat down with a drink and my newspaper. A couple of Leatherhead fans came in and we had a game of darts with the locals. The pub started filling up with football fans. Unbeknown to us the match between Fulham and Nottingham Forest had been called off, so all the Forest fans had decided to travel to the Leicester v Leatherhead game. This game, and Chris Kelly in particular, had gripped the imagination of the football public. It had gone one o'clock and I was feeling a little tipsy when into the pub came a contingent of Forest fans. We got talking and they explained the reason they were there. I started drinking with them. They were big drinkers and by the time we came out of the pub at 2.40, twenty minutes to kick-off, I was legless. By this time I had taught them the 'Kelly Shuffle', which was basically a freestyle conga.

We shuffled down to the turnstiles, abusing all the Leicester fans we could find. They were confused by the green and white and red and white scarves. The police looked at us warily. We immediately made straight for the bar, and I was just in time to see Jeff Stracey being marched around the pitch by a policeman. He had gone in the Leicester end and started fighting. As he was being marched around everyone was chanting 'Stracey, Stracey'. The policeman turned to him and said, 'Bit of a hero, are we son?'

He was locked in a police room under the main stand, but in a pre-match mix-up five minutes later he was let loose. He ran around the ground, came in our entrance and was in the bar with us before the kick-off. The Forest fans were impressed by Jeff and his incredible repertoire of flamboyant stories – which now had a ring of truth about them. Hadn't he been under arrest ten minutes ago? Yet here he was buying the beer. (Years later he escaped from prison and his description appeared on the front page of the London *Evening Standard* with the immortal words 'You won't take me alive!' In the event, he was captured in a pub blind drunk without a struggle.)

The first half and the fairy tale continued. Leatherhead went two–nil ahead with Kelly scoring one, making the other goal and generally tormenting Leicester without mercy. At half-time all that could be seen was the 'Kelly Shuffle' and the drinking (and spilling) of beer. In the second half the slaughter continued for a while. Kelly went round the goalkeeper and should have scored, but the ball was stopped on the line. I can still close my eyes and remember him going round the Leicester keeper and shouting 'Goal!' I don't think Leicester would have come back from three-nil down, but as it was this was the turning point of the match. Leicester scored, then destroyed a tiring Leatherhead, finally winning three–two. Nevertheless, the cheers at the end were all for Leatherhead. We left the ground disappointed but privileged to have witnessed one of the greatest performances ever by an amateur team.

Leicester fans approached Leatherhead fans in the street, shaking their hands and saying 'Great match' and 'Cor, what a game'. Had we won the match it is more likely that they would have been waiting to smash our heads in. In an instant, we would have been transformed from the quaint amateur team who had provided entertainment into the bastards who had humiliated and knocked Leicester out of the FA Cup.

A crowd of over 37,000 had witnessed the game and those present will never forget it. To this day everyone who was there talks about Kelly's miss. That night on *Match of the Day* on BBC 1 Jimmy Hill interviewed Chris Kelly. 'We'll be back next year, Jimmy,' said Chris – although sadly this was not to be. Nevertheless, Leatherhead have the proud record of never having lost to a professional team on their own ground, and have since beaten Cambridge United and drawn with Colchester United and Swansea City.

Leatherhead qualified for the FA Trophy Final in the year 1978. It was to be the swansong of an ageing team. Altrincham were the opponents. The buzz of a Wembley trip was felt by everyone, and we knew we would be up against Manchester's finest, both on the pitch and on the terraces. John Taylor had booked a fifty-two-seater coach to run from the Old Crown in Great Bookham, but every seat was taken within days and there was talk of booking another one. Food was organised for after the match (which of course we would win) so that we could picnic and party in the car park. The coach was due to leave at noon – high noon for those dirty Mancunians whom we would spank. The landlord opened the pub at ten and everyone was in there drinking like fishes. All the familiar faces were there: Monty, Jeff Stracey, Eric, Leggy. Jeff and I had borrowed brown butchers' coats from a shop up the road and had painted them in green and white. Midday came, but no coach.

'Where's the coach, John?'

'They may be a little late. Have another drink.'

Everyone kept drinking. One o'clock came; still no coach. By this time we were all too drunk to care anyway. At two o'clock John Taylor made a solemn announcement to a hushed pub: 'The coach is not turning up.'

'We want our money back,' was the general chorus, the full seriousness of the situation not immediately sinking in. Then it suddenly dawned on us that we would not be going to Wembley after all. I went outside and kicked John's car; a few other guys tried to turn it over. Some punches were thrown. John retreated into the saloon bar.

Sober volunteers were needed to drive cars and vans. One poor guy walking past with his wife was press-ganged into driving a car. 'Don't worry, love, it's only fifteen minutes' drive,' his wife was assured. He got home six hours later. Gareth Mills had a big Transit which he offered to drive, so twenty of us piled into the back. Gareth was the epitome of a Cockney football fan – to northern fans, that is: tall, always well dressed, good-looking, and always with a smooth hairstyle. We ripped the back of John Taylor's car open and took most of the beer with us, telling John in no uncertain terms, 'Be in the car park after the game with the food, or else.'

We were on our way, and a couple of miles and a few cans later we had forgotten about the inconvenience of the coach not turning up. We got to Wembley at three o'clock dead. By the time we got into the ground Leatherhead were one–nil down. They were trounced out of sight, eventually losing three–one to the best semi-professional team around at that time. I hadn't yet seen an Altrincham fan close to, but there were plenty in the stadium. It was amazing that I could see anything at all, because I had drunk so much.

Only half the stadium was being used, so the other half was empty. Someone bet me I couldn't get into the television gantry without being caught. I struck the bet and set off. The police and stewards chased me but I got around the empty section. However, when I got to the gantry the walkway had been removed to stop people walking across. So I swung across like a chimpanzee. The drop was at least thirty feet; in retrospect I must have been crazy even to think of attempting it. I reached the television gantry and promptly fell asleep. The next thing I knew the game was over and a steward was shouting at me to come down. I swung down and quickly slipped away before the police spotted me.

In the meantime, Jeff Stracey had been up to his tricks and had been singing his 'Harry Roberts' song when a policeman grabbed his painted coat. Jeff, quick as a flash, slipped out of the coat and ran off, leaving a bemused policeman holding a green and white butcher's coat. As well as this incident, Jeff had also been involved in a fracas in the car park with some Manchester United fans who were supporting Altrincham, and Gareth had been punched in the face for being a good-looking bastard!

I staggered out into the daylight. John Bramble approached me. 'Who won?' I asked.

'Altrincham, three–one.'

Some Altrincham fans then came along and began to laugh at me. I wasn't having that, so I ran at them. The next thing I remember is going backwards. I was being dragged along by my neck and being held in an armlock by Don Durban, an elderly sergeant-major type. He shouted back to the Altrincham fans, 'Don't worry, leave this one to me.' I really have to thank him for saving me from a terrible beating, and to this day I always buy him a barley-wine whenever I see him drinking in the pub.

John Taylor had turned up in the car park and had laid out all the food. It was an impressive spread, but within five minutes an almighty food fight had erupted with tomatoes being splattered on people's heads. The police turned up and were not amused. 'Where's your coach?' the superintendent asked.

Of course, we didn't have one, but some of the guys were in no fit state to be driving. 'It should be here soon,' we said. The police warned us and left.

Everyone headed for the cars. Peter Jackson, with his pals from Kingston, was in his black Hillman Hunter and drove straight out of the car park and into a car full of Pakistanis. They jumped out. Peter was well drunk. When the police turned up one of the Kingston guys accused the Pakistanis of reversing into him. The policeman, who had had enough, told both carloads to go home or he would arrest them all. Peter drove off, breathing a sigh of relief; the Pakistanis drove off livid, believing themselves to be the victims of racism.

We chugged off home, being refused service in every pub we stopped in for a drink. What a sight we must have looked, covered in beer, ketchup, mustard and relish!

That was it: the end of an era. We weren't to know it, but the decline of the team was to be rapid, and although some of the younger generation try to recreate the atmosphere of those heady days, it just isn't possible. What we had in Leatherhead was unique, a close-knit community growing up, travelling and fighting together. I would liken it to the friendship units that were formed and went to war together in 1914. The difference is that we returned.

3

Away from Home

Shortly after the Brighton match, Steve Mappin began travelling to the Arsenal home matches with Silly Vince and me. Steve had a fantastic sense of humour which, combined with a sharp wit, could invariably make you laugh. Everything he did was funny. How else would you describe a guy who damaged his knee cartilage through wearing a pair of Cuban-heeled boots on the terraces? With his frail physique and pale complexion he was never going to be a terrace thug. I loved going to Arsenal with him, but he was the biggest coward I have ever met in my life – a fact he will not argue with. He subsequently became nicknamed 'Shakin' Stevens' because he would literally shake like a leaf at the first sign of trouble. I get frightened, but I always try not to show it. He would not go to any ground where he considered violence might occur.

On our way to one match we were coming down the Tottenham High Road and got to the point where you turn right to go into the Park Lane end. A large group of Spurs fans was standing in the centre of the road outside an entrance, above which a sign in big letters stated 'Visiting Supporters Only'. Steve Mappin spotted them and went as white as a ghost. Silly Vince, who was wearing a tricolour scarf, was indifferent. I was wary. Why were they risking trouble standing there? Later I was to find out that they were testing the water to see how tough the Arsenal were. We walked past them and one of them shouted 'Rangers!' in response to Vince's scarf. Steve was fearful and all for going home.

We got into the ground without incident, but just before kick-off a huge mob of Spurs fans charged in, punching and kicking the Arsenal fans. We backed away; nobody fought back, so in came the Spurs fans again. An Arsenal fan next to me punched a Spurs supporter and his mate did the same. I joined in, thinking that perhaps everyone was going to fight back. A huge gap appeared around us. Steve Mappin said, 'I'm going for the teas.' That was the last we saw of him either that day or at any away game for three seasons! He still attended the home games, although even that almost came to a halt when some irate Newcastle supporters chased him at King's Cross.

On the day in question, however, Steve had not been a bad judge, because I later saw knives being flashed openly on the terraces. Arsenal fans were being threatened with stabbing. Silly Vince confronted one knife-wielding youth with a handkerchief.

'I'm going to stab you, you Arsenal bastard.'

'Not until I've blown my nose you're not!' replied Vince.

It lightened a tension-filled moment. After the game I stuck close to a policeman and then we slipped away. It was one of the few times I would have asked for police protection if necessary, this normally being a more dreadful crime than running.

Watching Arsenal became a chore. They had become a dia-

bolical team and in the season 1975–76 they were almost relegated. On the terraces they had lost all their credibility, and
people began to take liberties with them.

As the years went by it became the practice for the home
fans to wait for the away fans. This, coupled with stricter
segregation, led to more complicated infiltration manoeuvres. By the mid seventies the wearing of scarves, especially
at London derbies, was dying out, so the scarfless mob
would go on to the terraces in small groups. The problem
then was grouping together to become sufficient in numbers.
Sometimes this was achieved by means of a rallying chant of
the away team's name by a small group, but more usually it
happened as the home team ran out on to the pitch (the
home team normally ran out first). This would give the away
fans a chance to see who was cheering; a surge at the middle
usually caused panic and gave the away mob enough time to
group.

Another chilly March afternoon; yet another Chelsea v
Arsenal league match. Neither team could win the League,
but that meant nothing to the two sets of fans who would
turn up for the skirmish. The Arsenal fans had been invading the Shed end for the past four seasons, and this season,
1973–74, would be no exception. This was to become
known as the year of the yellow paint, courtesy of the
Arsenal fan who had a spray can of the stuff and spent all
afternoon depositing it over everyone's hair and clothes.

The Arsenal fans had infiltrated, and a few had massed in
the centre of the Shed. Just before kick-off trouble erupted
when a fight broke out between two small groups of opposing fans. A chant of 'Arsenal!' was the rallying cry which
drew other Arsenal fans into the fray. A brief flurry, loads of
punches thrown amongst the frenzied shouts. The Chelsea
fans in the immediate area backed off. It was all running true
to form: the Chelsea fans would stand off us as we took the

Shed. Although incensed, they would marvel at our nerve and courage and stay backed off until the end of the match when we would return home triumphant with another notch on our belts. Unfortunately the Chelsea fans forgot to read the script this year, and their repeated surges compressed the Arsenal supporters into a small pocket in the centre of the Shed. Without the police, who saved the Arsenal fans by setting up a protective cordon, I don't think any would have survived. Even the cordon didn't deter some Chelsea fans, who were literally climbing over the top of the police to punch their rivals. The superintendent realised that the arrest of one Chelsea fan would cost two bobbies from his thin blue line, so the attacks continued unabated while he waited for reinforcements. It would be the away fans' turn to retreat today.

'We've got you surrounded,' sang the Chelsea mob, which was countered by 'No Surrender' from the Arsenal fans – although, in reality every Arsenal fan was petrified and wanted out. No one cared about the loss of face a strategic withdrawal would bring.

Again the Chelsea fans surged forward like a wave, chanting as one, 'Ooh all together, ooh all together'. Those who were not in the front line chanted 'You're gonna get your fuckin' heads kicked in'. The fighting became more frantic as the Chelsea realised the Arsenal were going to capitulate. More paint was sprayed, which led to more irate policemen who got covered in it – but try as they might they could not find the culprit with the spray can. The last remaining Arsenal fans were glad to be led out long before the end of the match, and the Arsenal have never been in the Shed since. But it should be said that Chelsea, despite their reputation, are not a nasty crowd, unlike some mobs who are really vicious.

There is no doubt that a lot of people travel to away football matches just for the excitement and camaraderie they offer.

There is always a cross-section of fans on an Arsenal train, including older and younger supporters. The trains going to Chelsea away games would appear to contain a much younger element, and that is why they seem to get involved in more vandal-related violence. Travelling on a football train is quite a laugh. It used to be even better when you could take as much booze as you liked. But a few years ago an old by-law was invoked which made it an offence to consume or be in possession of alcohol on trains. This was originally brought into effect as a direct result of rowdyism on trains at the turn of the century.

Coming out of a train station was a tremendous feeling, with people charging everywhere, but it always amazed me how the mob would arrange itself into some sort of fighting order for the walk through a town centre, in case of a confrontation with opposing fans. There were three distinct categories within the group: front, middle and back. The front men were the tough ones, those who liked to charge and throw punches to make the other mob back off; they liked to feel the adrenalin flow. There were always a few shrewd people at the front who knew that could look good without throwing a punch, but generally the ones who didn't want to fight stayed in the middle, running to keep up with the guys at the front so they didn't get left behind. The real nutters brought up the rear, because that was where the real fights took place.

It is unfortunate that some people occasionally became detached and were picked on as stragglers. This happened more often after the match than before it, and it was worse at some grounds than others because of the distance between the ground and the station. Liverpool was one of the worst places for this. It always amazes me that the press dub Liverpudlians a friendly, fair crowd because whenever I have been to that city I have found them the exact opposite. It seems to me that they love nothing better than to set upon a couple of lone Cockneys and batter them senseless. Leeds was another example. The Leeds United fans, before the advent of mass bus shuttle transport between the ground and station, used to taunt the away fans about the 2½-mile journey with the chant: 'You'll never reach the station.'

The police took some time to get themselves organised for the arrival of football specials. Originally it was two bobbies pointing the way to the ground. Nowadays a train is met with dogs, horses and vanloads of policemen, although the return to the station is still a problem because of the huge numbers of people coming on to the streets at the same time.

Vince and I came out of the ground. We had drawn one–all. It had been just an ordinary League game but I had never been to Wolves before and had read of plans to redevelop the ground, so I wanted to go before it was done. (I can't for the life of me understand why redevelopment was necessary, because it looked a smashing ground.) We were in no rush and ambled along at the rear of the Arsenal fans leaving the ground. It was about fifteen minutes walk back to the station and the police were walking along beside us. We had to go under a main road and we walked down the steps to the subway. As we entered the tunnel the Arsenal supporters began chanting 'Arsenal!' All of a sudden came a roar of 'Wanderers!', and pandemonium broke out. We had become detached from the main body, there were no lights and no police, and we were getting beaten to hell. It was one of those moments when it's every man for himself. I put my head down and ran, pulling Vince through towards the light at the end of the subway. The police had turned up, and although the fracas had lasted ninety seconds at the most, it seems like hours when you are on the receiving end. When it is all over and you are safely on the train going home, then the sheer terror recedes; but while you are going through it the experience is indescribable, and no drug could possibly reproduce that same feeling.

For some unknown reason West Ham fans have always been regarded as fair. Do me a favour! West Ham was the only ground I ever went where, for five whole seasons, I never cheered Arsenal. I went in fear of my life – most Arsenal fans were too frightened to go there at all. When we played them at home they always came in the North Bank. In 1975 we drew in the FA Cup sixth round at home. They practically took the whole ground over and I think they outnumbered us in the North Bank two to one. I'm sure the whole of East London turned up that day.

For years after that West Ham fans would enter the North Bank to humiliate and terrorise the Arsenal fans. But everything moves in circles, and the last time West Ham entered the North Bank en masse I was fortunate enough to be on the terraces and in among the action.

It was Mayday 1982. My brother had returned from overseas and I offered him my seat, which he gratefully accepted. I clicked through the turnstiles via the Gillespie Road entrance and climbed the steps which led on to the terraces, but instead of the normal orderly procession of people filing up the steps there was an impromptu fight going on. The big scarfless group in front of me who were West Ham fans were faced with five or six young Arsenal fans led by a fit-looking bull-necked guy who was casually dressed with tracksuit bottoms tucked into white baseball boots. He was up on his toes punching and kicking everyone who tried to advance up the thirty or so steps.

'Come on, you East London slags!' he challenged them.

The West Ham fans charged at him like madmen, but along with his friends he repelled every attack. In between punches he would hold his arms outstretched to beckon more West Ham fans forward; palms flat, fingers moving back and forth inviting everybody to try their luck and their every failure was met with mocking tones.

'I thought you lot was hard. Who's next?'

That would cause more indignant attacks, but try as they might they could not get the Arsenal fans to capitulate. The West Ham fans, who numbered at least twenty, were thwarted for at least two minutes until the police turned up and everyone scattered, leaving the policemen standing, open-mouthed and clueless as to what had happened.

'Who saw anything?' shouted the police.

Everyone just shrugged and walked on, as if the whole incident hadn't occurred. It had been an unusual scene because normally the West Ham fans could walk in unopposed. Their hardcore thugs, the 'Inter City Firm' (ICF), had not yet arrived in force, although perhaps they had infiltrated in small groups. The mood amongst the Arsenal fans was strange. Small groups had been waiting at the two entrances to the North Bank for the past hour and a half to engage West Ham fans in isolated fist fights. This state of affairs prevailed until 2.50 when the two teams ran out on to the pitch, and as all the Arsenal fans cheered an orange smoke bomb was detonated in the centre of the North Bank causing absolute panic. The ICF made a dramatic entrance on to the terraces. About fifty of them charged down the terrace, punching and kicking the coughing and spluttering fans in their path. Terrified fans fled on to the pitch to escape the pandemonium. The ICF were causing havoc – but today, unlike in previous years, they were not going to have it all their own way.

I was punched in the face and retreated from the oncoming ICF. I had no idea what was going on, as I had been blinded by the smoke. Suddenly I felt myself being propelled forward, as were others alongside me, by people pushing from the rear. Shouts of 'Come on, Arsenal!' and 'Go at them!' could be heard. Guys ran past me and into the smoke, and their silhouettes could be clearly seen standing toe to toe slugging it out with the West Ham fans. More Arsenal fans joined the fray, myself included. It was fist and boot, but the ICF were backing away. A burly West Ham fan came bounding out of the smoke at me and I waited to hit him as he ducked under the metal barrier that stood between us. But before I could blink an eye, two young Greeks set about him, knocking him down. He hit the ground with a dull thud.

'Do him!' The boot went in. Other West Ham fans saw him go down and attempted to come to his aid, but a chant of 'Arsenal!' rallied the young gladiators and the Arsenal fans charged again. Normally the shout of 'West Ham!' would cause Arsenal fans to run, but today it was having the opposite effect. The ICF were getting set upon from all sides and only the intervention of the police saved them from total humiliation.

Something else happened that day which I think shocked a lot of West Ham fans: people who were sick and tired of them spoiling their day out finally snapped. Once such person was Steve Ashgate. Steve, a great Arsenal fan with an effusive attitude towards life and football (football and especially Arsenal meant everything to him), was the last person I would have expected to see throwing punches on the terraces. Plenty of people like Steve watch football intently, and one can often spot them in pubs around football grounds on match days expounding theories of their team's defensive weaknesses alongside the meaning of life. Steve entered the ground from the Avenell Road turnstiles just as the fighting broke out. He had just taken up his usual position when a group of fans came pushing past him.

'Steady on, mate,' said Steve.

'It's all right, pal, we're West Ham.'

Steve didn't say anything but without warning just thumped the first guy, who went straight down on to the floor. Steve, who is six feet and fifteen stone, thumped his friend who went the same way, and a third suffered the same fate before other Arsenal fans stepped into the fray to help Steve. When the police turned up they arrested the three prostrate West Ham fans, who didn't know what had hit them.

It was the police presence that saved West Ham that day. But the ICF had the final say. After the match an Arsenal fan was mortally wounded a hundred yards from the ground. It is one thing having a punch-up, but stabbing someone to death is another matter. No one was ever convicted for that murder, but the following season some young Arsenal fans were jailed for conspiracy to commit affray and jailed for between three and five years for planning a revenge mission.

The death of the Arsenal fan and the dramatic press pictures of the smoke bomb brought to public attention the existence of organised terrace gangs. The press and police found out what the guys on the terraces had known for a long time: that the ICF were a particularly nasty gang who liked to leave a calling card on their victims. 'Congratulations, you have just met the ICF' said the card. I think this practice stemmed from the film *Apocalypse Now* in which the crazy colonel played by Robert Duvall was seen doing the same to dead Vietcong.

This game exploded the myth of West Ham. The press had dubbed them fair and knowledgeable about the sport, nicknaming the team the 'Academy of Football'. If the reporters had stood on the terraces, then a nickname such as the 'Epitome of Nastiness' might have been a more likely title. The press generally don't have a clue what is going on, and papers like the *Sun* (the hooligans' bible) don't help. They glorify the thugs when it suits them and generally lower moral standards. They even did an article once on one of the ICF, making him out to be some sort of cult hero.

People reading this book may get the idea that a day out

at football is good fun only if it involves a punch-up. Not true, but you cannot take away the thrill that is associated with a confrontation at football, any more than you can take away the thrill of watching a horse cross the finishing line when you have money riding on it. Companies are now sending employees into forests with paint-firing guns, to see how they react under pressure. People even play stress games for fun and get a lot of enjoyment out of them. I am sure that the emotional feelings of these games and on the terraces are very similar, but the real difference is this: on the terraces there is no cop-out and the fear is real. Your split-second reaction will decide whether you go home unblemished or bruised and battered. Sometimes you think, 'Oh no, this isn't really happening to me,' but it *is* and you must react. People, who in everyday life have to perform monotonous tasks, who haven't got a paper qualification and never will have, come to life, making crucial and instantaneous decisions – which then inspires other fans to follow them loyally and obediently. It is a way of gaining respect.

A day at football is special, getting up, travelling, anticipating, having a drink and finally the football itself. The whole shooting match really. The match lasts ninety minutes although the day can last eighteen hours, but no football, no day out. You learn a lot about people when a fight erupts on the terraces. Normally reliable people, the sort who never let you down, just turn and flee. They run past you, their faces drained of all colour, every one with that same terrified look, lips tightly drawn and eyes fixed straight ahead looking for a sanctuary and an end to their nightmare.

Cup Final day in May at Wembley Stadium, with its twin towers and the emotive walk up Olympic Way, is the dream of every football fan who sees their team play in the FA Cup. Every cup excursion brings different feelings. Is this going to be our year? everyone would ask themselves.

The worst feeling for any fan is for their team to get

knocked out of the FA Cup. When the final whistle blows
and the other team's fans are cheering wildly you try to console yourself and fellow fans who are similarly distraught.
No matter what is said, the pain inside will not go away and
the sense of injustice and frustration stays with you for
weeks. It is especially hard getting knocked out of the semi-
final, so near yet so far. Only ninety minutes from Wembley.
Everyone thinks back to previous rounds when it would
have been preferable to be beaten. Losing a League game is
bad, there's always next week; but lose a cup tie and it's
twelve months to wait.

After Arsenal had lost to Sunderland in the 1973 FA Cup
semi-final, everyone stood in line feeling sickened. It is a
feeling that is a combination of butterflies and acute abdom-
inal pain that affects your whole body. People trotted out
excuses trying to make themselves feel better, but to no
avail. A busload of Sunderland fans arrived, got out and
started laughing at us. The Arsenal fans went berserk and
charged after them, catching a couple and thumping the
living daylights out of them. One look at the faces of the
returning Arsenal fans from the fracas told the whole story.
They had punched the sickness out of their systems.
Punching an opposing fan in the head after a defeat can't win
the game or totally exorcise the pain, but it sure does stop
you feeling as lousy as you did previously.

Every supporter has his most-hated rival team, usually
the nearest neighbour geographically, and losing to them
on the football pitch means a period of absolute misery.
Losing a terrace battle to your nearest neighbour means
total humiliation and taunting chants at future matches.
It is amazing how quickly news of a humiliation on the terraces
spreads along the hooligan grapevine. I even saw a hooligan
top ten once, written on a gate outside Spurs' Paxton Road
end.

*

'Go west, young man.' Well, I did so one Saturday – to Bristol, which as far as many Cockneys are concerned is real bumpkin land inhabited by buffoons who use the phrase 'ooh-aar' in every sentence. In 1976 Bristol City reached the First Division and beat Arsenal one–nil at Highbury. Thousands of Bristol fans travelled to Highbury; but the place to teach them a lesson was on their home ground, Ashton Gate.

Paddington Station mid-morning. The Bristol express was stationary, full of expectant Arsenal fans. A few people leaned out of the open windows making banal comments or giving gestures of recognition to other fans. Finally a squeak of brakes being released and the train jerked into movement. By the time the train reached the end of the platform the familiar sound of escaping gas from ring-pull cans could be heard as people started drinking. Word soon spread along the train: 'All in the Bristol end today', and sure enough, when we arrived in Bristol as a group of about two hundred we made our way towards the home supporters' end. We passed row after row of terraced houses exactly the same as any typical north London street, but to some of the group they were inferior simply because they were in Bristol.

'Look at the state of those houses.'

'Yeah, two up two down and an outside shithouse.'

'Every front garden is concrete.'

'Can't afford lawnmowers, can they?'

'I expect they still bath in a tub in front of the fire.'

'Leave it out, running water hasn't reached this year far west yet.'

The dialogue reflected the sense of superiority many of the travelling Cockneys felt. All that remained was to teach the locals a lesson in terrace manoeuvres.

'We're gonna show these halfwits the new way.'

'One shout of "Arsenal!" and this end will empty.'

'They'll talk about today for a long time.'

Everybody laughed and felt smug; nobody felt threatened. At last the turnstiles: here we go.

Click, click, click is a familiar sound to football fans. It is the sound of the turnstile moving around against the metal ratchet as you go through. It's always reassuring to hear the clicks because you know you have arrived at the main event; but on this day my own heart seemed to be beating as loudly as the turnstile. I was one of the first twenty or so to gain entry, and once through I was confronted by a sea of hesitant faces surveying us for signs that we were Cockneys. We had to infiltrate quickly or we were in big trouble. There seemed to be too many people milling around for comfort, and suddenly a shout went up: 'There's Londoners in our end. Do the Cockney bastards!'

I heard the sound of the fist hitting a face. People who ten seconds earlier had looked hesitant and nervous came forward in a human wave. We backed off and some of our group saw the futility of standing our ground and leapt back over the turnstiles. I couldn't see a way out and just concentrated on covering myself from the shower of blows. The guy next to me got kicked in the face and went down into the gravel. A girl ran up and grabbed his hair, pulling it violently while at the same time spitting at him. She was foaming at the mouth. 'You bastard!' she screamed.

Apart from the girl other people were queueing up to kick him, and the sickening sound of boots hitting his body could be heard repeatedly. It was indiscriminate and nasty: any part of his torso was fair game. One really vicious guy was trying to stamp on his face with the heel of his boot.

'Help me, they're going to kill me,' he pleaded, but no one could do anything. The other Arsenal fans on the other side of the turnstiles made no attempt to come in and help us, although I don't blame them considering the savage beating we were getting. A few pretended to try to come in, but it was only bravado.

I had retreated as far as I could and found myself penned in a corner between a tea hut and a concrete wall. I saw flailing fists and felt blows against my face. I gave up trying to block them and concentrated on curling up into a ball to give my attackers as little target as possible to aim at. Everybody was trying to punch or kick my head, and the sheer weight of numbers and frenzy of the attack saved me, for no one could get a decent blow in and they spent most of their energy kicking each other. I had my arms covering my head and my knees tight up against my chest, and my legs took most of the blows. I managed to glance up through my arms and saw an amazing sight. One Arsenal fan, whose name I later learned was Mick, was making a solitary stand of defiance. He had his back up against a wall and had about twenty-five guys in front of him all trying to give him a punch in the face. Mick would take five or six blows and then give one back, and he managed to send a couple sprawling on to their backsides.

I thought the nightmare would never end, but the police soon turned up and the Bristol fans scattered, leaving us to pick ourselves up, dust ourselves down and get ejected by the police. Everyone tried to leave with as much dignity as they could muster, but the leers and catcalls rang in our ears.

'Go 'ome, Cockneys.'

'You won't try that again.'

'That taught you flash bastards a lesson. You won't come 'ere again and try to take the piss, will you?'

We all walked out of the ground, even including the guy who had taken the severe beating. The police marched us up the other end and as we were shepherded out of the gate a few more home fans charged forward to throw punches at us.

'If it wasn't for the coppers you'd be dead,' sang the Bristol fans as the police escorted us to the opposite end where we had to pay again to gain entry. Some of the fans who hadn't taken a beating cheekily asked for free entry. 'Come on, you're not going to make us pay again, are you?' But the police would have none of it.

After the match the police escorted us to the station and put us on trains back to London. Plenty of us had black eyes, grazes and lumps coming up on our heads, but by Paddington Station Mental Mickey's last stand had given us the self-awarded status of a moral victory. We laughed and joked on the way home, mostly thankful we had survived (even though it is hard to laugh with bruised ribs). To add insult to injury, we had lost the match two–nil.

The FA Cup tie against Notts County had been put forward to 2.30 p.m. to prevent a clash with Notts Forest who were also playing at home that day. (The two grounds are less than half a mile apart – it seems ludicrous that they do not share.) Going to away games is a great way of meeting people, and it never bothered me if I had no one to travel with because I would always meet someone. All I ever needed was the standard equipment: a supply of beer, pack of cards and newspapers. Today I met John Evans and a few of his friends and teamed up with them. John and his pals were a great bunch. They were funny and knowledgeable about music, politics and football. As I was sitting talking one of the group leaned over and spoke to me.

'Excuse me, but are you one of those types that smashes up trains, then runs out of the station punching people in the head?'

He said it in a tone of voice that signified he would be most unhappy if I behaved in that sort of manner. Everyone was quiet, waiting for my answer.

'No, of course not,' I replied seriously.

'Well, we are!' he shouted out, and with that everybody burst out laughing. It turned out that they were not troublemakers but just loved a bit of fun – great people to travel away with. They told me that I would be welcome any time in the Plimsoll Arms, and Steve Mappin, Vince and I began to drink there, having many memorable nights out after big games.

Every town has its nutters and hard men, and every football team is much the same, although it would be a struggle to find a punch-up in Norwich. I had an enjoyable day out there once. We knew there was going to be no trouble so the day out was simply a football excursion. Everyone arrived in a pub off the early train shortly before midday, and at three o'clock some of the Arsenal fans were so drunk they couldn't get to the game. One guy was fast asleep on the stairs that led to the toilet. The landlord, who had taken a great deal of money, was reluctant to phone the police in case anyone got arrested for being drunk and disorderly, so he threw out everyone who could walk and let the rest sleep where they fell.

Ipswich, too, was always a good day out. I can never understand anyone wanting to fight there, as they are such a friendly crowd. There was one occasion, though, when we almost got into trouble. Four of us had gone to see Arsenal play in a League match one Easter, which Arsenal won two–nil, and in the process deprived Ipswich of the League title. Dave Fincham, Phil Mamara, Steve Mappin and I were there. Dave was a real boozer, and his wife wouldn't let him go out very often because he always ended up legless. We had gone to Ipswich and found a pub that was open. (A lot of pubs had started closing on match days because of trouble.) We had had a lot to drink before the match and had been playing spoof, which is a game where you guess the number of coins in someone's hand.

After the game we headed back to the same pub. Dave invited two girls along and was telling them really them funny stories about when he had worked on the roads as a digger. At about seven o'clock the girls' two boyfriends turned up and Dave had to go some to talk his way out of that one, particularly as he was getting on really well with one of the girls. When a few more friends of the boyfriend turned up we thought it was best to leave, so we decided to go to a disco-pub called the General Gordon. This turned out to be full of Ipswich fans, but that didn't bother us. Once inside we started playing spoof again. A couple of real country bumpkins came over and asked if they could join in. One of them was as thick as two short planks and proceeded to buy six consecutive rounds of beer, the forfeit for losing the game. He kept saying things like 'Ain't you Cockneys clever' and 'What a great way to get drunk'. The comment which sent us into hysterics came after he had bought the sixth round: 'I don't think I've quite got the hang of this game!'

I couldn't stand up any more. We rolled about the floor, and to make matters worse he asked, 'Have I said something funny?'

In the meantime, his mate had phoned us a taxi because the others in the pub were going to lynch us for being Arsenal fans. We were having such a good time we hadn't noticed. The taxi turned up and we left. The others jumped into the cab but I just left the car door open and said to the driver, 'As soon as I get in, speed off up the road.' He looked bewildered, but he would soon understand. I walked back through the door of the pub and shouted 'Arsenal, Arsenal!' I then raced back to the taxi and we sped off. We looked back and about fifty guys were piling out of the doors to fill us in.

All the way back to the station we kept repeating what the village idiot had said and bursting into renewed laughter. But when got there we stopped laughing abruptly: we had missed the last train. We had a council of war and decided to nick a car. Steve Mappin had the first bit of luck in a multi-storey car park. He managed to open a door – but failed to notice that the car was balanced on bricks! It went on like this. We were totally flummoxed, until Steve tried another door which opened. Inside the car were loads of cassettes lying around. Steve locked the doors and said, 'That should stop anyone stealing these. People around here are so trusting!'

We gave up. Phil and I headed for a police station to try to get a cell for the night, and Dave and Steve decided to sleep on the train. At the police station the sergeant said, 'Cell? No chance. Go and wait in the waiting room with the other two.' I duly went into the waiting room and there were two Arsenal fans lying on the benches, both in their early twenties. One of them looked terrible; the other woke up. 'Oh, I thought you were someone else,' he said. He explained that his friend had been arrested for drunk driving and they were waiting for him to get out. We were offered a lift back to London. About an hour later the sergeant came in and said, 'Your mate's been bailed out and gone home.'

We found out later that the sergeant had told him that no one had waited for him, so he shot away. I think it was the sergeant's way of getting back at us for giving the police a hard time. Nothing else to do but get our heads down in the waiting room. I didn't sleep at all, and the chap who looked ill was sick all night in a metal mop bucket which stood in the corner. After every vomiting session he would mumble 'No more Bacardi'. We left the police station at about five o'clock and walked back to the station where we met Steve and Dave. They hadn't slept all night either. The journey home was dreadful, but every time I felt low I asked the sickly one if he'd like a Bacardi! The big drawback of travelling away is coming home on draughty, uncomfortable trains. They always seem to take an age to arrive, and the buffets are invariably shut when there is a trainload of football fans.

'Open up this bloody buffet,' shouted an Arsenal fan. The train had just pulled out of Manchester after a cup tie at

Bolton, and it was full of Arsenal fans. Its departure had
been delayed by an hour, for what reason I don't know, and
neither, apparently, did British Rail. We were about fifteen
minutes out of Manchester when one guy lost his temper
and, sensing there were no police on board, kicked the door
to the buffet car. It burst open and in he went. Inside was a
fully stocked British Rail Buffet. He helped himself, and
others soon followed. It wasn't planned – everyone had been
waiting in line to pay; but now it was free it was help-your-
self time. By the time I arrived there was nothing left, just a
load of young blokes cooking a huge urn of porridge. Every
time the train lurched, the porridge slopped everywhere. It
looked like a bomb had hit the place with broken plates,
food and rubbish strewn about.

I went back to my seat and someone came down the train
selling beer. A guy about nineteen years old sitting opposite,
who was nothing to do with football, had a can of lager
which he had bought from an off-licence and he swapped it
for a can of Special Brew which he opened up and started
sipping. As we thought, the train had no police on board,
and it just chugged along towards London. It pulled in at
Kettering and a British Rail official stood on the platform
open-mouthed at the devastation in front of him. Off he
scurried to the phone. The train set off about thirty minutes
later with a large contingent of police on board determined
to make arrests. Up the train they went. Nobody had moved,
and no one, of course, even knew there was a buffet on the
train! A couple of people who were sitting surrounded by
food were pulled to one side, but that was it. Even they
stood there proclaiming their innocence. A police inspector
came into our carriage and spotted the can on the table in
front of the guy opposite me. He approached him and picked
up the can.

'Where did you buy this from, son?'

'I bought it in an off-licence in Manchester.'

The police inspector looked at him with an 'I've got one at last' look. 'How many off-licences do you know that sell Special Brew with a British Rail logo on it?'

'I don't know.'

'I do, sonny. You're nicked.'

The police officer was well pleased, and he announced loudly to the rest of the carriage: 'When we get to Euston we will hold this train until all the guilty parties are brought to book.'

The train pulled in at Bedford, where British Rail staff were running up and down the platform. They ran up to the window of our carriage. 'Everybody off. Quick, clear the train.' The police officers were dumbfounded and tried to tell the British Rail staff that there was an investigation in progress, but the railwaymen told them in no uncertain terms, 'Listen we've got a bad derailment down the line and we need heavy lifting gear pronto, so this train must be cleared in five minutes.'

No one needed to be told twice, and we were off the train. Everyone was herded on to another train on another platform. The police gave up the investigation and we all got back to London about an hour later. The poor guy who had been arrested was still white when we got there. In the end no one got arrested for the Great Train Buffet Robbery – and no one ate the porridge, as far as I know.

Most away games start the same: you meet at the station stocked up with provisions and newspapers. It may turn out to be just an ordinary day, but sometimes something happens to leave the trip etched in your memory for ever. One such day was Middlesbrough away in the FA Cup.

As soon as the draw was made Steve Mappin decided that it was too far north. Anyway, he said, 'My passport is out of date!' But Vince and I were not going to miss this game. We set off on the 9.15 train loaded up to the teeth with alcohol, as were plenty of others on the train. It was a four-hour train journey and 4 to 5,000 Arsenal fans were making the trip. The North-East's football fans had a reputation for being quite nasty, but that seemed the last thing on everyone's mind especially a big group that was centred around the buffet bar and was really knocking back the booze. Everybody was singing: 'We're gonna win the Cup.' Vince and I met a guy on the train, a real character who was wearing a pair of bright yellow patent-leather shoes. He was wafer thin, had blond curly hair and talked incessantly about the disadvantages of being born in Middlesbrough. He constantly tried to imitate a Teesside accent but only succeeded in sounding like a caricature Pakistani, which made everyone laugh even more.

As it was a special train it was not due to stop, but it pulled into one station en route for an unofficial stop. As usual everyone who could find a window stuck their heads out to chant 'Arsenal!' and hurl abuse at the locals. A few rival fans waiting for trains looked on warily and stood well back, and as the train pulled out they were hit by a barrage of empty beer cans and shouts of 'Wankers!' The train pulled into Middlesbrough at about one o'clock and everybody piled off and ran towards the exit. We were the first of four special trains, and a large contingent of police was present to escort the Arsenal fans the mile or so walk to the ground. They had chosen a route that passed through the edge of a shopping precinct. As we walked by, groups of Saturday shoppers looked at us as if we came from another planet, while at the same time groups of Middlesbrough fans waited to confront us – although they soon scattered when Arsenal fans walked towards them. A lone newspaper seller standing on a street corner had placed a sheet of paper inside the metal grille on the front of his stand which read 'COCKNEY INVASION'. One fan wanted this, but as he tried to open the front grille to steal it the newspaper seller hit him. A group of four fans set about the elderly man and one of them threw a bundle of newspapers across the pavement into the road. The old man held on to the front grille and saved the headline sheet, but at the cost of thirty or forty newspapers.

I didn't want to go to the ground at one o'clock so Vince and I slipped away from the escort and went for a bite to eat before we made our way to the match. We had purchased tickets for the game back in London because we had been told it was an all-ticket game, but I noticed it was possible to pay to get in. We turned right to enter the road where our entrance was and a large group of Arsenal fans was standing in the middle of the road arguing with each other.

'Come on, let's run these tossers.'

The tossers in question were a group of Middlesbrough fans standing provocatively in the middle of the road fifty yards away. Three Arsenal fans led the way and the group moved forward as one. At twenty paces the Middlesbrough fans shouted and insinuated they were going to charge, but the Arsenal fans didn't flinch; they roared back and broke into a run, causing the Middlesbrough fans to retreat down the road. The Arsenal supporters walked back to their entrance laughing – they had run the Middlesbrough fans without a punch being thrown. We entered the ground and went on to the terrace which ran the length of the pitch. Vince and I went and stood near a fence which separated us from a large open terrace. I noticed that on the track between the terrace and the pitch were two special screens made of canvas and wood laid on top of one another. I turned to Vince.

'I wonder what they are for.'

'I dunno, but they sure are funny-looking stretchers,' he said, with a shrug of his shoulders.

At about 2.45 some Middlesbrough fans came up to the fence and started spitting at their rivals, who returned the compliment. We moved away from the fence and the next moment the teams ran out on to the pitch. I still had one eye on the terrace to my right and noticed pieces of brick coming over. I turned towards the terrace to watch and catch the pieces of brick. The next things to come over were full cans of lager that had been slightly opened. It was not difficult to catch them and lob them back. By now the Arsenal fans were surging forward to try to get at Middlesbrough fans. Then I saw something which took a little while to comprehend. A dart flew over and stuck into the top of the shoulder of an Arsenal fan standing near me. It had embedded itself quite firmly and must have been thrown from quite a distance. I shouted out 'Darts!' as did other people. I was wearing a flat cap and I pulled it off and managed to catch one in it. I threw it on the floor – but now I wish I had thrown it back. I took my eye off the terrace for one second and a dart flew past my face. I heard an agonised cry and as I looked around I saw a ghastly sight: a young man had a dart sticking through the centre of his eye. He instinctively put his hands up to his face, not realising the dart was there.

The police forced their way on to the terrace and slotted the canvas screens on to the top of the fence. They slotted on so easily that it was obvious this had happened many times before. I forced a way through the crowd and helped the poor fan to the front, pushing people roughly out of the way. I jumped up on to the track and helped him out. A policeman ran over to stop us getting on to the track, but when he saw the dart sticking out of the man's eye he stood dumbstruck, white-faced and open-mouthed. He called for an ambulance man and helped to lead him along the track with a couple of his friends. I turned to the open terrace and standing in front of me were two Middlesbrough fans laughing at the plight of the injured Arsenal fan. I was incensed. I couldn't believe I had just seen someone lose an eye. What sort of person would throw a dart into a crowd when the chances were that it would hit a face? I held on to the rail and swung my boot at their faces hoping I would connect and break a jaw, but I missed. Vince shouted out 'Old Bill, Ginger', and I realised I was going to get myself arrested. I jumped back on to the Arsenal terrace and made myself scarce. The few Arsenal fans who did jump into the Middlesbrough section were ejected and arrested.

When Arsenal were three–one down I left the ground with Vince and ambled back to the station. We bumped into two other Arsenal fans, who walked along with us. As we got to the edge of the precinct one of the fans, whose name was Willie, seemed nervous despite the fact that he had an impressive physique and looked capable of fending for himself.

'If I were you I would take your scarves *off*,' he said.

'Why's that?' asked Vince.

'Because I have heard that around here they don't attend the game but hang around outside the ground waiting for small groups of fans like us.'

'Well, if these slags want action, then they can have it,' replied Vince.

Willie was about to speak, but Vince stopped him in his tracks.

'Listen, shitpants, if you feel uneasy about walking along with us then walk on your own, otherwise shut up and be prepared to fight because we have no intention of running.'

This made Willie and his mate even more nervous, and they dropped back twenty paces. We walked on and as we went past the end of the precinct and into the station forecourt, Vince turned round and shouted, 'It's all right, frightened Willie, you can come out now.'

After the game, which Arsenal lost four–one, a big mob of Arsenal fans came out and stormed around the town looking for the Middlesbrough fans who had indulged in the mindless dart-throwing violence. Meanwhile, the stragglers were beaten to a pulp. The Cockneys had invaded and paid a terrible price.

During the return journey we saw Yellow Shoes again and he was sporting a real shiner of an eye. He said that a middle-aged man had approached him in a pub toilet and said, 'Only London poofs wear yellow shoes,' then belted him. I suppose it wasn't funny, but everyone roared with laughter and so did he. I never saw him wear yellow shoes again, but the nickname stuck. Tragically, he died some time later as a result of heroin addiction.

Throughout the whole journey I couldn't get the sight of the dart sticking out of that man's eye out of my mind. It haunted me, and on Monday morning I sat down and wrote a long letter to my MP. I was extremely critical of the police handling of the match and the way we had been positioned between two groups of Middlesbrough fans. I felt that the existence of the canvas screens proved that missiles had been thrown before – so why weren't they in position before the darts were thrown? The replies from the Home Secretary and the Chief Constable were a whitewash in my opinion. The police even informed me that the darts I had seen were in fact nails stolen by Arsenal fans. I know what pub darts look like – I had even caught one in my hat – and the gruesome sight I witnessed that day will be with me for ever. As a happier conclusion, the *Sunday Times'* inside track column reported the incident and it was from there that I learned that the Arsenal fan, by a miracle, did not lose the sight of his eye.

The next away-game of note was in the following season, 1977–78, when we were due to play Liverpool in the League Cup semi-final first leg at Anfield. I had unhappy and frightening memories of that city from five years earlier, but as soon as the draw was made I knew I would be there. The fact that I had heard dozens of stories from various supporters about violence at Anfield made no difference. The general press opinion of the fairness of Liverpool fans has obviously been formed from the safe distance of a cosy press box. Most newspapermen have never been on the streets, and when they do see street-level violence they are horrified and can't understand it.

I travelled up to this game on my own, having been split up from my friends at Euston after trying to get a free trip on the first-class Travel Club train and been thrown off. I had Vince's ticket with me to sell, for he had decided that he couldn't afford it. Steve Mappin had decided he hadn't the time to learn a foreign language (Scouse) and anyway he still hadn't got a new passport! I have never sung so much on a train journey in my life, before or since. Expectations were high because Arsenal had emerged from a bad period with an exciting young team, and Liverpool, although they were the best team in Europe, would be no match for us, of course.

We got to Lime Street Station and everybody jumped out, chanting; no Liverpool fans would mess with this mob. Everyone was surging out of the station and jumping on buses, but I was weary and couldn't stand the pushing, so I went round the corner and stepped on a bus which would take me past the ground but wasn't full of shouting Arsenal fans. I settled down in the bus with my newspaper, listening to the comments of the Liverpool fans about how many Cockneys were in town. The bus pulled up right outside the Kop end, the famous home end of Liverpool fans. This is the end with no gangways, so people who need to go to the toilet piss on each other's legs. (Scousers call it a 'hot leg' and are quite proud of it.)

As the bus pulled up, loads of faces peered in. They were looking for a lone Cockney to beat up. It sent my mind back five years. This time I had no scarf on, but nevertheless I wasn't going to take any chances. It is amazing, but when you go to football it is possible to tell where someone comes from by the way they dress and their general demeanour. I decided not to get off the bus and stayed there reading my newspaper. At the next stop I got off and walked back to the ground. Arsenal fans had been given half the Anfield Road end, the opposite end to the Kop, and I walked down the long road full of terraced houses that runs behind the seats. I made a note of the way back to the bus stop for after the game. When I reached Anfield Road I decided to sell Vince's ticket. I was approached by four young Liverpool fans who were about sixteen years old.

'Got any tickets?' they asked.

'I've got one.'

'How much?'

'Fiver.'

'Stuff it, Cockney.'

That annoyed me, but I wanted to sell it. 'How much then?' I asked.

'Quid.'

'Piss off, I'd rather burn it.'

The cheeky little Scouser then pulled out a box of matches. I pulled the ticket out, tore it up and rammed it right in his face so that the pieces blew everywhere.

'You burn it.'

Another Arsenal fan had heard this, and he slapped one of the Liverpool fans hard round the side of the head. 'Go back to your own end,' he said. They disappeared fast.

I entered the ground and saw all my friends: John Evans, Trevor Smith and others too numerous to mention. Trevor (TC to his pals) was the most outrageous guy who has ever travelled to a football match. His dress sense was weird to say the least; he was the doyen of the King's Road set, and every new fashion would be sure to feature in Trevor's wardrobe. Meeting him at a football game was like welcoming a long-lost brother home from the wars: all hugs and back-slaps. In fact, lots of football fans behave like that; it seems that football can unite people in a unique way.

A bar is a great place to get information, and according to the pub stories the Liverpool fans had been willing to mix it outside before the game. The word going about was that Everton fans, too, had been causing trouble for Arsenal. A guy who had been thumped by four young Liverpool fans came into the bar. I started laughing, wondering if it was the same four I had just had words with. The guy tried to knee me, but all he got for his trouble was hot tea in the face and a 'Piss off'. He walked off, shouting, 'I'll have you lot,' but he was all talk.

The game was good and Arsenal scored first. However, Liverpool equalised then scored a late winner to win two–one. Still, there was always the second leg. As the Arsenal fans left the ground, everyone seemed nervous and made an effort to stick together. The truth of the matter was that no one had a clue how to get back to the station. Outside in the narrow streets it was chaos. I shouted, 'Turn right!', and a large group of Arsenal fans followed us. There were Liverpool fans milling around everywhere, just waiting, but not having the bottle to attack. We should just have gone straight into them for having the cheek to stand there.

We turned right into the road leading up to the Kop, the rows of terraced houses silhouetted against the night sky by the one remaining street lamp that had not been smashed. The road looked dark and forbidding. I heard a roar and the Arsenal fans in front of me turned back. I could see fear and. panic on their faces. People around me were shouting 'Stand', but the Liverpool fans who had been waiting had found their courage now that they realised we weren't going to do anything. Fighting broke out everywhere. Trevor Smith was alongside me and in we went, punching and kicking. Other Arsenal fans joined in. When a fight erupts like this you just go in, and hope that everyone else does the same.

For a while it was the Liverpool fans' turn to feel fear. All around us they were backing off, each man with a look on his face that said 'please don't punch me'. But then the retreating fans began to advance, and I suddenly realised that only Trevor and I were fighting. It was time to run – we were marked men. I ran straight through a hedge into a front garden and then cleared two more gardens. I didn't even look behind.

When I came back into the road further down, I saw that the Liverpool fans were murdering the Arsenal, who were scattering everywhere. I was so frightened I could hardly breathe, let alone think. I decided to strike out on my own and head up the street towards the Kop and the bus stop. It was a risk, but perhaps the Liverpool fans would not suspect a lone person walking into them. I went back round the corner and a Liverpool fan walked up to me.

'Cockney bastard!'

I kicked him right in the balls and down he went. I just kept walking, and miraculously no one hit me. Fear gripped every part of me, and I swore to myself as I prayed for my nightmare to end that I would go to church every week if I came out of this one. I carried on up the road and saw one Arsenal fan getting kicked all over the pavement. I couldn't help him alone, so I walked past. It was every man for himself. – Sorry, mate!

I walked with a purpose as if I knew where I was going avoiding eye contact, just looking straight ahead. The road was full of people bumping into each other because it was so dark. On a wall on the left was a group a young Scousers trying to spot Cockneys in the crowd. I practised my Scouse accent under my breath, but my mouth was so dry I wouldn't have been able to say a word. As long as I was not forced to speak I would survive. I saw the light at the end of the road and as I got there I came across a parade of shops. A soon as I emerged into the light of the main road I was immediately spotted as a Cockney and pointed out. Nowhere to run. I was standing in the middle of the road and a policeman walked up to me and said, 'Move out of the road.'

'No.'

He came closer and said, 'Move, or I'll nick you.'

'Thanks very much, I'll accept that because there is no way I am walking anywhere to get a hiding.'

A plain-clothes policeman walked over and said that he and a uniformed officer were walking my way and I could follow them. Off they went, so I followed. But twenty yards down the road they received a radio message and ran off, leaving me on my own again. I shot down a side road, went round the block and came back on the main road. I saw a bus stop about fifty yards up the road and went for it. I walked past an Arsenal fan lying stabbed in the road. Then I saw a big group of Arsenal supporters at the corner, so I walked up to them and we exchanged stories about what had been happening. Suddenly a fight erupted again. I saw a knife flash and moved fast; some Liverpool fans with blades had moved in. Everyone scattered in all directions, and I ran down a side street. I looked back. Someone was down, but it wasn't my problem; mine was survival. I turned left and saw John Evans.

'What's been happening, Ginger?'

'It's bad,' I said.

'What are we going to do?' he asked.

'There's a bus stop up the road. If we make out we are locals then we should be okay.'

We went back up to the main road and met up with another couple of young Arsenal fans. I told them to take off their scarves and stick with us. We got to the bus stop and stood there. Behind us stood a derelict house, and in the garden were empty bottles of all descriptions. I went into the garden and picked up an empty quart bottle of cider. I ripped the inside pocket of my sheepskin and stuffed the bottle into the lining of my coat.

It was about this time that a Turkish guy and his family came along the road. He was in his late twenties and built like a brick outhouse. He had an 'Arsenal and Proud' T-shirt on, and although it was cold he had removed his coat and jumper which his mother was holding. He looked mad, and as we stood at the bus stop his mother told me what had happened. As they were leaving the ground she had been struck, and since then her son had fought every Liverpool fan he had seen who wanted trouble. He also wanted everyone to know that he was an Arsenal fan. The bus turned up and we got on and went upstairs. We had only been two stops when the burly Turk threw off two Liverpool fans for bad language. I felt safe now, with my bottle and my new-found Turkish friend.

The bus pulled up opposite Lime Street Station and that left us with fifty yards to go. The Turk jumped off with his family and walked away down the street. There were Liverpool fans waiting around everywhere, but I pulled out the bottle and put it just inside my coat. Anyone who tried it now would get a nasty surprise. I turned to John Evans and said, 'Take no crap from anyone.'

As we walked towards the station a group of Liverpool fans stood across the pavement, blocking our way. I got to within five yards of them, pulled out the bottle, smashed the end on some railings and said, 'The first one to try it is scarred for life.' Their smug expressions, which had said 'You Cockneys are going to get some' changed instantly to nervous friendly smiles. One of the group, who had his anorak hood pulled over his head just above his eyes, pulled his hands out of his pockets and held them out wide. He opened the palms of his hands to show us he was hiding nothing.

'We weren't going to have a go at you, honest.'

'Well, back off then and there will be no trouble, will there,' replied John with a sneer.

They soon backed away and as we walked into the station I threw the jagged bottle into a waste bin. Inside the station there were Arsenal fans everywhere with bloody noses and worse. I saw a friend of mine called Richard with his mate Bill who had been struck above the eye with a bottle; he would have a nasty scar there for the rest of his life. Richard had been beaten up and had his coat stolen. One of them had even tried to take his shoes. I had heard stories of Liverpool fans stealing clothes from well-dressed rival fans, but now I had seen it with my own eyes. It was Richard's fashionable clothes that had caused them to be spotted as Cockneys. In retrospect, I think the Liverpool and Everton fans set out that night systematically to attack as many Arsenal fans as they could. It didn't matter that they had won the football match. This was violence for the sake of it.

Years later I still haven't forgotten that night. I once saw a Liverpool fan get chased at Chelsea. He ran into the road, was knocked down by a taxi and broke his leg. I felt no sorrow, and inside something said 'Good'. On another occasion I saw an Everton fan savagely attacked on the London Underground by some Millwall fans, who hit him with an iron bar. When they had finished and jumped off the tube he vomited and lay motionless, covered in sick; yet although I was shocked I could find no pity in my heart.

In the return game against Liverpool at Highbury I went into the Clock end along with a lot of other Arsenal fans to get our revenge, but the cowardly Scousers knew what would be waiting for them and the few who did turn up were well protected by the police. To make matters worse, the game finished with no score. So Arsenal were eliminated on aggregate. I stood in the street outside Highbury feeling sick, along with 40,000 other Arsenal fans. But seven weeks later we were at Wembley for the big one – the FA Cup Final.

The previous week I had seen Leatherhead lose three-one. Today I was to see Arsenal totally outplayed by Ipswich and lose one–nil. After the game a good number of men sat in the mud outside the ground crying uncontrollably. Football is an emotional game. As Bill Shankly said, 'It is not a matter of life and death; it is more important than that.' I fully endorsed his comment. But the following season, 1979, Arsenal went back to Wembley and beat Manchester United three–two in one of the most memorable finishes ever seen at Wembley. That meant European opposition and European away matches.

4

Europe with Arsenal

In my football travels I have much preferred watching Arsenal abroad to watching England. For the most part people are keen on the football aspect when watching club teams, whereas some so-called England fans seem to spend most of their time falling about drunk. This doesn't ignore the fact that English club football fans have been involved in a lot of serious disturbances over the past decade or so. But often the problems have been caused not by the football fans but by the idiots attracted by the continental excursion. The English FA, along with EUFA, the European governing body, have resolved to discourage football fans from travelling to away matches in Europe.

This first European match I decided to attend was in East Germany, where, in 1979, Arsenal played FC Magdeburg. I had booked up to travel with Arsenal Travel Club which was run by David Dryer. His nephew Russell was installed as the manager–organiser of the Travel Club. I don't know why it is, but people always seem to treat the average football fan as sub-human, someone who will put up with any discomfort. This trip to Magdeburg was the worst organised trip I have ever been on in my entire life. The people in charge were totally incompetent.

We left Arsenal at seven on Monday evening to travel down to Felixstowe to make the crossing to Belgium. We arrived in Belgium at seven the next morning, (which with the time difference became eight), and we were supposed to arrive in Leipzig at seven on Tuesday evening. The coach pootled along and I discovered that its maximum speed was only 50 mph as it had no rollbars. The modern Belgian and German coaches were shooting past us. An Arsenal supporter who spoke fluent German had a map. He gave it to me and I worked out that we would be lucky to arrive at midnight. I confronted Russell Dryer and the other stewards, but was accused of being a troublemaker.

'What do you know about travel?' one steward asked.

'A lot more than you do, mate,' I replied. I went back to my seat seething at their attitude.

All the fans on the coach thought I was joking when I told them how long it would take, but as the hours ticked past tempers became frayed. The border crossing into East Germany went very smoothly, thanks to the German-speaking Arsenal fan. We were told not to bother changing any money as you could buy anything with sterling. Some of the guys on the coach were loaded with East German money. When Arsenal had played Locomotive Leipzig in the previous season they had sold souvenirs and badges of Arsenal FC for about five times their value (the East Germans would pay a lot of money for English football souvenirs). When they got back to England with the East German Deutschmarks they found out they couldn't cash them, so they saved them and waited for Arsenal to play in East Germany again. Their patience had been rewarded.

We arrived at the hotel in Leipzig, which was opposite the railway station – a very impressive building. It was two o'clock on Wednesday morning. The steward told us all to remain seated, but by now everyone had had enough. One guy stormed up to the steward and for a moment I thought he would hit him; but he pushed him out of the door and shouted everyone off. We all piled out, thankful that at last we could stretch our legs. We were told that food was laid on at a hotel down the road and that we had to be on the coach by eight in the morning because we had a long way to travel to Magdeburg. That was only five and a half hours away, so I quickly went for something to eat and then retired to bed. I was shattered. I had to share a room with someone else and a supposedly twin-bedded room in fact had a small double bed. The guy I slept with snored all night. We had a seven o'clock alarm call and went down for breakfast. At eight Russell Dryer came into the breakfast room and said, 'Hurry up, you lot.' A torrent of foul language was hurled back at him. If he hadn't walked out he would have been lynched.

The coach journey to Magdeburg was interesting because we had a pretty young German girl on the coach as our guide. We were all offered work in the German Democratic Republic and the usual 'ways-of-making-you-work' jokes were bandied about. We arrived at Magdeburg at about one in the afternoon, and pretty soon the whole coach was doing a roaring trade in Arsenal souvenirs with the young East Germans. It was noticeable that when the police told the youngsters to go away, they did.

The steward made his way to the main hotel in Magdeburg to pick up our tickets from the club, and it was then that I realised the real reason why we had undergone the horrendous journey to Leipzig then back to Magdeburg: the club had not wanted the football fans to stay in the same hotel as the players. This is the sort of mentality most football fans have to put up with. The club wants your money, but heaven forbid they should ever have to speak to or socialise with the fans. There may have been a logical reason, but look at the geography of East Germany and then tell me I'm wrong. In addition, the coach parked well away from the hotel and we were politely asked not to go near the players. The previous season in Leipzig Terry Neill, the Arsenal manager, a man I respect, had come across to the fans' hotel and personally thanked every one for travelling. But this is the exception, not the rule. And even when you actually meet footballers, the majority are thickos whose conversation revolves around money.

We drove off to the ground and went in. It was a pretty drab place, rather like an English Third Division ground, and Arsenal easily won the tie. We had been promised a few hours sightseeing in East Germany, but after the game we were asked to sit on the coach so that numbers could be counted, and then the coaches sped off. I should have just not returned to the coach, because they wouldn't have gone without me; they were frightened that they wouldn't get back across the border without the correct number of people. We sped (50 mph) back to the border and crossed at Marienborn. In West Germany we stopped at a restaurant and I left the bus; I couldn't stand one more minute on that coach. I later discovered that they stopped for a couple of hours in a little Dutch town which everybody loathed.

I vowed never to travel with the supporters club again, and when I finally returned to England I phoned up the club and spoke to Ken Friar, the Arsenal Secretary. I complained that the Travel Club was not affiliated to ABTA (Association of British Travel Agents) and therefore a disgruntled customer had no redress. The club was not interested, but I understand that the subject of the Travel Club was raised at the annual shareholders' meeting. The following season Arsenal quietly dropped David Dryer Travel and ran the club itself. I wonder how many other businessmen are attached to football clubs and are short-changing football fans.

Arsenal were now in the quarter-finals, in which they disposed of Gothenburg five–one. I had been intending to travel to Gothenburg but decided I would save my money for the semi-final, in which Arsenal were paired with Juventus. The first leg at Highbury was drawn one-all, with Arsenal scoring a last-minute equaliser. Everyone except me was convinced that it was curtains for Arsenal. I told Steve Mappin that Turin was the place to be, but Steve decided he didn't much care for pasta. Vince was skint, so I decided to travel on my own.

I set off on the Tuesday morning from Victoria on the first boat train·which left at about eight in the morning. I spent an enjoyable afternoon in Paris, from where I was catching the overnight train to Turin leaving at 8.40 p.m. It was due to arrive in Turin at 7.00 the next morning. I had a marvellous meal in Paris and settled down in my carriage for the journey. A French girl joined me and suggested we draw the blinds and stretch out to stop other people coming in; that way we would get some sleep. I agreed. No one came into our carriage and I slept till about 3 a.m. when I was woken by singing and dancing. There were about thirty Arsenal fans on the train and they had been partying since Paris where they had spent Monday night sampling the French whores. At the Italian border the customs officers informed us that Juventus would win two–nil, but we were having none of it.

The atmosphere was great, although quite a few French people couldn't understand the noise. A carriage door would occasionally open, a head would stick out into the corridor and someone would shout out something in French (keep the noise down, I presume). 'Piss off, you onion eater,' a typical reply would be, followed by a chorus of 'Arsenal, Arsenal, we're gonna win the Cup'.

We arrived in Turin buoyed up and convinced of our superiority. One of the fans, Ollie, walked out of the station with his Arsenal flag and a little Italian street urchin grabbed it and ran off. Ollie was a big Arsenal fan and I often saw him at the ground, but he had a horrible lisp and used to spit when he talked to you. His mate had the biggest nose who ever watched football: Solly was his name. I nicknamed them the 'gruesome twosome'. But aside from these minor disabilities they were good guys. All the Arsenal fans hung around the station listening to Ollie slagging off the Italian nation because he had had his flag stolen. At about nine o'clock the Arsenal fans who had travelled down the night before met up with us, so now we totalled around fifty. We went into a café for some food, but I saw an Arsenal supporter steal some money from the tip tin so I left with two other Arsenal fans. We ate, then spent an enjoyable morning walking around Turin. I already had my match ticket but my two companions didn't. It had been said in the newspapers back in England that the game had been sold out for a week, but we were approached by Italian touts who charged us the equivalent of £5 for a ticket. Later, in the town, we were given tickets by Arsenal fans who had managed to buy seats.

We went into a bar, and as the owner didn't like Juventus he bought us lots of beer. Kick-off time was still about two hours away, but around the stadium the streets were filled with people going to the match. In England everyone turns up about thirty minutes before kick-off – but not in Turin that night. The Italians are crazy about football and are always convinced they are going to win, and as we walked down to the ground locals would come up and shout at us, '*Juve, Juve, due–zero*', they were so worked up about the match. Turin is a fine city and I really enjoyed my day. It has beautiful wide streets and lovely architecture, the people are very friendly and the supporters of Torino, who share the stadium with Juventus, went out of their way to make us more than welcome.

I entered the ground after being searched by a policeman

(*carabiniero*) with a tear-gas gun. Inside the stadium, which is a giant concrete bowl, I felt a little disappointed for it was not as plush as I had expected. There is a running track between the pitch and the edge and a moat between the edge of the terraces and the running track with quite a drop to deter people from invading the pitch. I decided to stand away from the bulk of the Arsenal fans. There were between 50 and 75 fans who had made their own way, plus about 150 who had come with the Travel Club. About an hour to go to kick-off, and the ground was full. The ground was split into three sections. The side we were on, where the terracing spreads around to the area behind the goal at the far end, is the popular end for Juventus supporters. Just to our right is a fence and this section spreads around one end to the area of seats. On the far side is the seat and terrace area which runs the length of the pitch, and this is separately sectioned off.

During the first game at Highbury, Tardelli, the Juventus midfield player, had been sent off and remarks made by Terry Neill, the Arsenal manager, had been blown up out of all proportion by the Italian press. At Turin, behind one goal was a big banner which read 'NEILL THE DOG'. Terry Neill brought the Arsenal players on to the pitch and the sight of him sent the Italian fans wild. They had been relatively unconcerned about us up till now – after all, they were completely convinced that victory would be theirs. They needed only to draw nil–nil or win to take the tie, and they had only ever lost one home European tie in their entire history. We were a bit of a novelty, but now some Italians began to throw cans of Coke at us or stand on the barrier shouting insults. One particular Italian fan stood on the fence screaming at us with his eyes bulging and saliva coming out of his mouth – a frightening sight. But mostly the Italians seemed to like us A few Arsenal fans scaled the fence to enter our section and every time one got over the barbed wire the Italians cheered loudly.

A group of Italian fans around me had brought in with them a lot of what I thought was wine; it was being passed round and it reached me. I took it and as I drank everyone cheered delightedly. It was very strong. The Italians loved it, and their shouts demanded that I drink some more. Every time I swigged at the bottle there were more cheers. I was really glad to pass it on, as my throat was burning. I had thought it was wine, but I'm sure it was a lot stronger.

The teams came out and the scene before kick-off was the most incredible sight I have ever witnessed at a football match. One end was completely lit up by red roman candles. All around firecrackers were going off and every Italian was shouting '*Juve, Juve, Juve!*' You couldn't hear yourself think. An Arsenal supporter turned to me and shouted, 'If we win this game it will go down as one of the all-time great victories.' Looking around the ground at the Italian faces, I had to agree. The passion and emotion could never be expressed on paper; you had to be there to feel it for yourself. I thought, 'I wonder what they will be like if we win.' At that moment I don't think any one of the Arsenal supporters could have contemplated victory. I could see why the Italians had such a fantastic record.

The game started and Arsenal, playing controlled football, quietened the crowd. Arsenal had to score a goal, but with ten minutes to go, although Arsenal were pressing hard, the goal did not look like coming. The Italians, thinking that they had won courtesy of the goal they had scored at Highbury, started making a lot of noise. Arsenal had played magnificently, but were going out of the Cup. A minute to go, and Rix crossed to the far post. A header. GOAL! Arsenal fans erupted; the Italians were stunned. Normally I would go berserk, but on this occasion I just stood there. The final whistle went and Arsenal had won. The Italians were obviously disappointed, but the ones who had given me the 'wine' before kick-off all came over and shook my hand.

Some were in tears, but they still applauded Arsenal from the pitch.

The Arsenal fans stood cheering as the stadium quickly emptied. However, the younger Italians were not so magnanimous. They surged around to where 200 or so Arsenal fans were standing and began to throw bottles, cans and lumps of wood from discarded flags. Everyone retreated up the steps, forced back by about a thousand young Italians. The riot police just stood on the pitch watching; I suppose they would have fired tear-gas if things had got too out of hand. We had women and young children among us. Some of the Arsenal fans armed themselves and charged down the terraces. The Italians backed away, and this gave us a temporary respite. Everyone started arming themselves with bottles and lumps of wood – I got a good piece about eighteen inches long in my left hand and half a Coke bottle in my right, and I stuffed another Coke bottle in my pocket. Everyone else made the same preparations. We advanced slowly, and when we were about fifteen or twenty feet away someone shouted 'Fire!' A barrage of bottles hit the Italians.

'Charge!'

We surged forward, but the Italians ran like dogs. We walked back up the terracing thinking that was that, but the Italians regrouped about fifty yards along the terraces and began to advance again. We repeated the exercise.

'Fire!' 'Charge!'

This time the Italians backed off only a short distance. We held our ground at the top of the steps. They advanced slowly but surely, throwing cans and bits of bottle – but I saw the same look of uncertainty on their faces that I had seen on Leatherhead's fans years earlier at Millwall. I spotted a young Italian about twenty years old wearing a leather jacket; he seemed to be some sort of leader, so I decided he was the one for me. A roar went up, and down the steps we went into the mass of Italians. I felt the crunch of flesh and bone as my bit of wood hit a skull. The Italians retreated and a large body of Arsenal fans chased them along the terraces, whacking them on their backs and kicking them up the backside. I went towards my young Italian prey and hit him with a sharp left hook. He stumbled backwards down the terrace and I quickly moved forward and spun him round, grabbing his collar and the back of his trousers and at the same time running him down the terraces. I ran him into the wall and banged his head on the rail, quickly picked up his legs and bundled him over the rail and down into the moat. The drop at that point was about eight feet. As he hit the ground the Italian riot police set about him with their truncheons.

I went back up the terraces and saw an Arsenal fan getting the worst of it against three Italians. I came up behind one of them and punched him right in the kidneys. He let out a loud yell and I struck him hard on the side of the head. Other Arsenal fans moved in and the Italians backed away. The riot police appeared on the terraces and shepherded the Arsenal fans down into a tunnel which led down some steps to the exit. The remaining Arsenal guys, myself included, brought up the rear, making sure that no stragglers were left on the terraces. I entered the exit tunnel and walked down the steps. The Italian riot police had stopped everyone halfway down and were standing guard at the front, while we were standing guard at the rear. Our bodies were still pumped up with adrenaline and as we talked our tongues went as fast as our hearts. The fight we had just had hadn't lasted more than five minutes, but we had given the Italians a real lesson. Not only that, we were in the final of the Cup Winners' Cup.

As we stood there talking I was roughly pushed up against the wall. I turned round to see the chamber and barrel of a gun which was up against my temple. I remember thinking how small the bullets must be. Two guys were standing in front of me, both with guns, and were searching me, although neither wore a uniform. An older female Arsenal fan walked up the steps and remonstrated with them. They finished their search and walked down the steps. I grabbed one of them and asked, 'What was that about?' He said something in Italian and a senior uniformed officer walked up the steps and explained to me what was happening. He told me that the police had received a radio message that a tall ginger-haired man had been spotted with a gun, and that was why they had detained me in such a way. I thanked him for the explanation. So much had happened in the last ten minutes that it took until the next day for it to sink in that it had been a real gun pointing at my head.

The riot police held us for about fifteen minutes. They formed up at the front to escort us back to our coaches. I tagged along because it was a mile and a half to my hotel, which was in a dark back street near the station. We walked along, the riot police nervously fingering the triggers of their rifles which had tear-gas grenades fitted to the end of the barrels. Young Italians were hanging around spitting at us and hurling abuse. The women in our group were very frightened. 'Do you want some more?' challenged one Arsenal supporter, walking towards a group of Italian fans standing about thirty feet away. They backed off. The riot police didn't like the Arsenal fan doing this, and insinuated they would give him the butt of the gun if he did it again.

We reached the coaches – one of them had had its back window smashed. I decided to go back to the airport with the Travel Club coaches, as it seemed too dangerous for a ginger-haired Englishman to risk walking the streets of Turin. Out in the darkness were mean streets full of vengeful Italians, and I didn't intend to give anyone the chance of attacking me. I tried to persuade the coach driver to drop me at the railway station where I would take my chances with the hundred yards left to go. At last I had a stroke of luck: a taxi driver was on one of the coaches talking to the driver, and he offered me a lift back to the station at no charge. Even better, his taxi was parked about a quarter of a mile down the road and the coach would drop us there.

The three coaches pulled away in sequence, but as they did so, from out of the darkness ran four or five young Italians. One threw a stone at the window and the others jumped at the windows, foaming at the mouth like rabid dogs and unable to contain their anger. Their eyes bulged from their sockets. It was a terrifying sight. Football incites many passions, but in Italy, as in South American countries, it is like a religion. Everybody condemns English football fans, but I have never seen any English fans react like that. The Italians were full of hatred and saw nothing wrong with pelting women and children with bottles and cans. How would you react? We defended ourselves from this unprovoked attack and I myself am proud of the way the Arsenal fans rallied round to protect innocent people.

The coach stopped and the taxi driver and I disembarked. There were Juventus fans walking along, but we were too quick getting out and into the taxi for anyone to react and have a pop at me. I felt safe in the taxi, and the driver kept saying to me, 'Arsenal number one. Liam Brady king.' (Liam Brady, of course, was the Irish genius who played midfield for Arsenal and in a short while was to leave Arsenal and sign for Juventus. The funny thing is that if Juventus had won they probably wouldn't have signed Brady.)

The taxi pulled up outside the station but on the wrong side. I had to get round to the other side and I didn't fancy walking. I gesticulated to show the driver what I wanted, but the silly Italian thought I wanted to pay him. All he wanted to do was shake my hand. 'No money. Arsenal number one, Brady number one.'

I gave up and said, '*Italia numero uno.*'

I jumped out of the taxi thanking him in French and German because I didn't know the Italian for 'thanks'. He smiled broadly and left, still shouting out of his window, 'Arsenal number one, Brady number one.'

I was on my own now. I saw some other Arsenal fans walking into the station. I wondered how they had got there so fast, but I didn't stop to talk to them. I crossed the road quickly; the streets were wide, but I had no intention of hesitating. I remembered the first rule – look confident and keep moving – so that's what I did, pulling up my collar as I moved along. I felt good. The adrenaline was flowing; my legs were moving automatically, and every sense was on red alert. I came to the corner; my hotel was thirty yards down a dark side street. My heart was in my mouth. How I wished I had been staying at the hotel on the corner which was a little more expensive but a lot safer. I moved down the dark street looking from side to side, and at last I reached the hotel. I was here, safe. I turned at the entrance and looked up to the Turin night sky. I held my arms aloft and shouted, 'Yeah, we did it!' It was the first chance I'd had, because everything had been so frantic after the final whistle. Grinning broadly, I walked into the foyer of the hotel and up to the reception desk, collected my room key and went into the bar. Four Italians were sitting at the bar looking glum. I ordered a beer.

'Don't worry, lads, it's not the end of the world,' I said.

They looked at me impassively, and I just walked up the stairs with my beer to my room. How I wish I had been with Steve and Vince, because that bar would not have shut that night. But it's hard to celebrate on your own. I lay on the bed and shut my eyes; the goal came back to me time and time again. I was still pumped up, but there was nothing to do except lie there, although I couldn't sleep much. I would have loved to walk the streets bar-hopping, singing and dancing, but since I valued my life I lay there reflecting on the day and thinking how wonderful life was. I finally slept a little, and in the morning when I left the hotel I bought an

Italian paper. It had six pages devoted to the previous night's match, and I also learned that our opponents in the final would be Valencia of Spain. This was to be held in May in Brussels.

A few months later England were due to play in the European Championships based in Turin. As soon as the England fans arrived, the Italians started attacking them. I left Turin behind after only one day, but count that as one of the best days I have spent at a football match. I experienced the full range of emotions, and lived to tell the tale.

There was no doubt about it, 1980 was going to be a momentous season. Arsenal had reached two cup finals but it was Brussels that everyone talked about. It is every football fan's dream to see his team play and win a final on foreign soil. Arsenal had lost the FA Cup Final on the Saturday at Wembley, but after the game everyone had sung 'Brussels, here we come.' Some guys had even had bags of clothes at the game – they were leaving on Saturday night.

We had a gruesome foursome travelling. Steve Mappin said that he loved sprouts, so he was on board! Tarby Wales, Vic Watson and I made up the four. (Tarby was so called because he looks like Jimmy Tarbuck.) Vic, who is the world's greatest chatterbox, asked me to organise the match tickets and hotel accommodation, so I duly got the tickets and a list of hotels. We set out on Tuesday morning first thing from a hotel in London. We were travelling by coach, hovercraft, and a coach to Brussels. A few lagers were drunk, but nothing to excess, and Vic's constant chattering made everyone laugh.

The coach journey to Brussels was uneventful except for a toilet stop when everyone used the facilities but didn't realise that a small payment was expected. My limited French came in handy, for some of the Arsenal fans had drunk a lot and their graphic language and general dislike of foreigners almost caused an incident. I just wanted to get to Brussels on time, so I organised a small payment and received a beer from some of the guys on the coach for my trouble.

When we got to Brussels, some guys headed straight for the nearest bar and started drinking. We got into a hotel for a wash and brush-up. After a bite to eat we were ready to head into the city centre to see what the night would offer. We walked down into the red-light district – where else would football fans drink? Brussels was expecting 15 to 20,000 Arsenal fans and its population was a little bit nervous. I didn't blame them, for English football fans had a bad reputation. We found a smashing bar called L'Eldo, so we went in and started drinking. It was around seven o'clock and it was quiet. The owner of the bar and his wife were young. Steve, who is one of the most polite people I know, chatted away to the owner's wife, while I tried to convince the owner that I was a disc jockey of some repute, for he had a record console in the corner. He laughed but explained that the disco was only in operation from Thursday to Sunday. Nevertheless, he put on some good English music for us.

We decided to make this bar GHQ, and as the night progressed more Arsenal fans who were bar-hopping came in to join us. The talk was about how many Arsenal fans were in town and what was happening. We were very popular in our bar, and when two Arsenal fans came in very badly drunk, Vic told them they should be ashamed to be English and not able to hold their drink. Another Arsenal fan then entered the bar; he thought he had been drinking for twelve hours, but didn't know where he was or what hotel he was staying at. We went through his pockets and found a card, so Steve pointed him in the right direction – but he just staggered into another bar. Next, a couple came into the bar and sat down at the next table, and Steve started chatting to them. The woman was elegantly dressed and reasonably attractive. Eventually the couple got up and left, but later, on a walkabout in the red-light district, we spotted her in a window. The guy she had been with in the bar was outside; he was her pimp. In the bar he had been chatty, but now out here he was on business and wanted nothing to do with our small talk. The woman waved at Steve and beckoned to him, but Steve shied away.

'It's all right, love, I'm only a looker,' Steve explained.

When the woman realised that Steve was not a customer she cut him dead; the conviviality that had occurred earlier counted for nothing.

We moved on and drank the night away to the background noise of police and ambulance sirens. Young Arsenal fans were battling on the streets with the local gangs and pimps. We were in one bar and some young fans came in to announce that there had been a stabbing. We headed for home at about three o'clock, ready for the big match on Wednesday. The next morning *Le Soir* carried a picture of a drunken skinhead, along with the night's statistics: thirty-nine Arsenal fans (but no one from Valencia) had been arrested for disturbances. The streets were full of Belgian police, but an uneasy calm lay over the city.

We took up residence at a bar in a street that was packed with Arsenal fans along its entire length. It was a scene being reproduced all over Brussels. Every time a pretty girl walked down the street the cheering could be heard for miles. Everyone was sitting outside on the pavements, and more people were turning up by the hour. A rumour flew about that a ferry had been turned back at Ostend because of the trouble caused by Arsenal fans on the boat. At about midday the first Spanish fans arrived. They were friendly and there was no trouble between the Spaniards and us before the game.

I went into the bar just as Steve was leaving. He told me

that a Belgian guy was very annoyed because every Arsenal fan was looking at his girlfriend. It certainly was very hard not to stare at her. She had swept-back light-coloured hair, a perfect figure, beautiful boobs and a lovely smile. I came out of the toilet and smiled at her. Her boyfriend, who had a moustache and looked like a San Francisco gay, said something in Flemish. 'Bollocks,' was my reply.

I returned to my seat outside the bar. Suddenly I saw the boyfriend come charging out after a slightly overweight Arsenal fan who ran over to our table and said, 'I only smiled at the girl.'

The Belgian stood outside the bar and started shouting at us. He put his right hand on his left bicep and clenched a fist, and then he put up both his fists. I think he was saying he would fight the best man among us.

'I'm game,' said Tarby. He stood up and took off his glasses.

'Leave it out, Tarby. Let him come to us,' I said. Vic stood up and imitated exactly what the Belgian had done. The boyfriend stepped forward, bent over and patted his bum. This time I think he was saying we were cowards (shit-outs). Well, that was it. All four of us got up and started patting our bums with about forty other fans chanting, 'Bummer, Bummer'. The Belgian stormed back into the bar, grabbed his girl and walked up the road, still shouting. The cheers went up. Everyone was wolf-whistling the girl, who looked even more stunning being dragged up the road. The riot police walked over and looked at us. They confiscated a football from two young blokes, then parked their van full of riot police in the road so that they could watch us.

'What do you think they're thinking?' someone asked.

'Probably can't believe how much of this crap lager we're drinking.'

'Oi, barman, got any bitter? This stuff's shit.'

The intellectual level of the conversation dropped as each

hour passed. It became apparent that a lot of people were there for the beer; the football match was incidental. We headed towards the ground, travelling by tram. Everywhere you looked there were Arsenal fans drinking.

The Heysel Stadium in Brussels is next to a giant model of an atom. It is called the Atomium, and was built for an exhibition. Inside is a museum, and in its grounds is a funfair where a lot of the Arsenal fans were enjoying the rides. We arrived at the ground at about forty minutes from kick-off. The ground itself was in a disgusting state of repair, and the fence at the back of one of the terraces was only six feet high. Every Arsenal fan had a ticket, and anyway you could pay on the gate. We had the best seats in the house and we took our places, with me sitting in the seat next to the gangway. Across from us were the Valencia fans. They kept throwing firecrackers which exploded with a mighty bang. Tarby went over and said to a Spaniard, 'Don't throw them near us.'

The stadium filled up. Sitting in front of us were a guy and his girlfriend who were called Andy and Jill. Next to them were two Arsenal fans who had had a lot to drink. Their language was disgusting and they behaved terribly. Andy asked them to tone it down, but they just laughed at him. When the teams came out that seemed to calm them down, but after five minutes' play they started again. I will not reveal their words, but it was embarrassing to listen to. Andy asked them again to cut it out. The Arsenal fan next to him turned round and spat in his face. But Andy was not having that; he stood up and punched him right on the nose, breaking it, I think. Blood spurted everywhere. Andy dragged him into the alleyway and hit him again, putting him on the ground. The police came down and the Arsenal fan walked up the steps with his friend to an ambulance. Goodbye to him! Five minutes later the guy's friend returned and sat next to Andy and his girlfriend. Andy said, 'I'm sorry, but he gave me no choice.'

'No problem, mate, no hard feelings from me.'

We all settled down again, but about a minute later the Arsenal fan who had just seen his mate hit jumped up and viciously struck the unsuspecting Andy. He hit him above the eye and split it wide open. Blood pumped out of the eye and all over his girlfriend. He hit him about three times, then tried to run away. But I had seen enough. I jumped up and he didn't even see my fist hit him as he ran up the steps. I felt his nose break and once more blood spurted everywhere. The police ran down the steps, grabbed him and dragged him away while Andy had to be restrained from giving him a real beating. Andy and Jill also had to go to hospital; he needed stitches above his left eye. There was blood everywhere, and the Spaniards could not understand what was going on. Fifteen minutes gone and the score was two broken noses and one split eye. None of the injured returned during the game.

About twenty minutes later a firecracker exploded under our seat and totally deafened us. I turned round and saw the culprit. I walked over and dragged the Spaniard out of his seat and held him for the police, who were running down the steps. 'Here he is, officer, throw him out,' I said. But the police grabbed me instead, dragged me up the steps and threw me out of the ground. I suppose they had seen me belt one guy and manhandle a Spaniard, so they thought they knew who was the guilty party. They chucked me out of the ground at the same time as another Arsenal fan, who promptly tried to walk straight back in. The Belgian police went mad and manoeuvred him into a van driving up the road. About five minutes later he returned, breathless.

'What happened?' I asked.

'They chucked me in the van, drove me up the road a little way, gave me a beating and threw me out. So I ran across the tram tracks and here I am.'

At that moment the van came back around the corner; he

had beaten it back. We ducked out of sight and nipped in another entrance. The doors at the back of the stand were open and we soon conned our way past the policeman on duty. We still had our ticket stubs, so we flashed them and in we went. I went back to my seat and the other Arsenal fan to his. The riot police had dealt with their man and we were all happy.

At half-time everyone went to the toilet. In Belgian football grounds, as in most toilets on the Continent, they have female attendants who expect you to pay to use the facilities, which are lovely and clean. I think it is a good idea because most toilets in English grounds are disgusting. It was such a funny sight to see those Belgian women shouting abuse at the English football fans, grabbing them and stopping them going into the toilet. The practice of most football fans at half-time is that anywhere will do, so the wall outside the toilet became the urinal. What the female attendant must have thought of the English I dread to think. It was one of those embarrassing moments when you don't know where to put your face.

There were more incidents in the second half and no goals, not even after extra time. A penalty shoot-out. It was too exciting for me so I went and stood outside the ground with a few other Arsenal fans. We knew the score from the cheers of the crowd. Rix missed the last penalty and Valencia won the Cup. I was sick. I shook hands with a few Spaniards, tears in my eyes, but thousands of Arsenal fans went absolutely mental. They charged into the Spaniards. Outside the ground there were assaults and cars getting smashed up and turned over. It was not a pretty sight, so we headed back to our bar for a drink – but it was shut, as were most bars in the city. I was not surprised. Eventually we found a bar away from it all and had one drink. A car drove past us with Spanish flags hanging out of the windows. From further down the road I heard the smash of glass. All through the night in our hotel room the sound of sirens wailed. Defeat is a bitter pill to swallow, but the reaction of the Arsenal fans shocked me. I thought we were better than this. Our proud reputation as good, fair fans was being destroyed by drunken yobbos.

The next day everyone headed home, shell-shocked, leaving the people of Brussels to get on with the job of clearing up the mess. How could we have lost on penalties? Since that day every Arsenal fan I speak to remembers the defeat in Brussels as their worst moment ever. But I find the post-match violence the worst aspect of the whole thing. Biased I may be, but I had hoped that Arsenal fans were above that sort of thing, and that only other clubs encouraged that kind of following. But it seems that the potential for violence is in everyone. Apparently, as soon as an English team gets to a European final then the day-tripper liberation army is on the loose. The celebrations start as soon as the train sets out from Victoria. Perhaps this has something to do with the fact that we are an island race, but whatever the reason, as soon as some people cross the Channel they change. The people of Brussels were left shaking their heads in astonishment, unable to comprehend the aggression of a nation's youth – particularly when it was the same nation they had so admired for liberating them from the Nazis. This type of behaviour is due to a sort of working-class tabloid press mentality, a 'Brits are best' approach. To make it worse, I had not expected it. Seeing Arsenal fans involved in drunken mayhem was sickening for me.

5

Chelsea

Zigger – Oi!
Zagger – Oi!
Zigger Zagger, Zigger Zagger – Oi, Oi, Oi!

This was the oft-heard chant at all football grounds in the sixties and seventies, but every time I hear that chant, and also the song 'Liquidator' by Harry J. and the All Stars, it reminds me of Chelsea at the Shed end and the incredible sight of thousands of people clapping in unison to an old reggae song. The area I lived in, Leatherhead, was, like all South London areas, staunch Chelsea. If you were older there was always Fulham, but Chelsea, with its surfeit of public houses and trendy players, was the team to follow if you were young, macho and vibrant. Loyalty to Arsenal and other teams was passed down from father to son, but as the average age of Chelsea's fans never seems to increase I can only presume they all retire to the allotments at thirty-four. I, too, gained an affinity for the team at an early age when a friend of my father's regularly took me to the matches after my mother's death.

Chelsea fans are the most optimistic I have ever met, tending to think they are doing better than they really are. They also have a tremendous away following and have been involved in a lot of incidents over the years. This has gained them something of a reputation. When they travel away the supporters all seem to be young, so when something does happen it tends to get out of hand as everyone joins in. Chelsea slipped into the Second Division in the season 1974–75. The big crunch match was down at White Hart Lane, home of Spurs. Chelsea and Spurs both needed to win to stay up, so the battle on the pitch and terraces was always going to be ferocious.

I don't know what happened, but Chelsea got murdered that day. The match was made famous by the referee Jack Taylor, who was a Wolverhampton butcher, walking out on to the pitch while warring fans were fighting a frenzied battle on it. It was generally reckoned by Chelsea to be the blackest day in their terrace history. Reputations are important, and relegated Chelsea set about regaining theirs in the Second Division. By the time they had returned to the top flight they had a ban on their supporters attending away matches. It became the rage down at the Bridge to wear a T-shirt (if you had the physique) or a sweatshirt with the words emblazoned on the front 'You Can't Ban a Chelsea Fan'.

I wrote a letter to MP Dennis Howell, who was then Minister of Sport, asking how he proposed to stop Chelsea fans purchasing tickets from Arsenal FC when they played at Highbury. The reply from the Department of the Environment was comical.

24th August 1977

Dear Mr Ward

I have been asked by Mr Howell to reply to your
letter of 13 June expressing your concern over the
possible continuation of the ban on Chelsea
Supporters attending away matches for the 1977/78
season. I apologise for the delay in replying.

The Minister's Working Party on Crowd
Behaviour met recently to discuss arrangements for
the new season. As you probably know, the ticket
restrictions imposed on both Manchester United and
Chelsea football clubs at the end of last season have
been modified although all away games involving
these clubs will be all-ticket occasions. The Working
Party also strongly advises all clubs to consider all-
ticket arrangements for potentially vulnerable
matches. Both home and away clubs have been asked
to sell tickets only to registered supporters such as
season-ticket holders, shareholders, members of
official supporters' clubs and *loyal supporters* whose
good behaviour can be guaranteed .

It is appreciated that the decision taken by the
Football League, after consultation with the Football
Association and Mr Howell, to make both
Manchester United and Chelsea football clubs' away
games all ticket, and to exclude their followers from
the terraces for the remainder of last season,
adversely affected many genuine supporters.

The problem of football hooliganism is being kept
under continuous review, and the Minister is
determined to overcome this problem and make all
parts of football grounds safe so that true supporters
like yourself can enjoy watching their football and
not be intimidated by a hooligan minority.

Thank you for making us aware of your views and
I hope you have an enjoyable season watching
Arsenal.

Yours sincerely,
R.J. LAWRENCE

Whatever else a hooligan is, he is certainly a 'loyal supporter'. Chelsea fans would turn up at grounds and gain
entry in droves. There was coverage of a game on the television news one night, and as Chelsea scored the camera
switched to the terraces where about two thousand Chelsea
fans were going wild. They were supposed to be banned.
How can the police, whose duty it is to keep law and order,
let two or three thousand football fans roam town centres?
No, they did the logical thing: they let the fans in where
they could keep an eye on them and after the game herded
them back to the station and put them on trains. Good rid-
dance, but thank God we got away with it. One only has to
remember what Chelsea did to Luton town centre on the
two occasions they went there while in the Second Division.

Luton Town is a dump of a ground, unfit for football fans
in my opinion. Luton had the inspired idea that season of
employing stewards to keep order and liaise with the police.
These stewards would keep unruly fans in line and chuck
out troublemakers. They would also wear pink coats,
because it was a neutral colour and wouldn't provoke
anyone. The police, who tend to provoke crowds, would
merely provide back-up – or so someone thought. The guy
who dreamed that up must have had his brains in his pants
that day. The stewards got nicknamed the 'Pink Panthers',
and the system worked well until Chelsea hit town and the
Pink Panthers started on a Chelsea fan who was being
thrown out. Hooligans respect the police uniform and most
people realise that if it's a fair cop, all right. But with the Pink

Panthers, no way. Chelsea fans went berserk, and pitch invasions and fights took place. The trip back to the town station saw the mass destruction of the town centre. Shops were looted and a train was set on fire.

The following season Chelsea went up to Luton once more and did the same again. It was said that one guy who didn't like football but had a fetish about smashing shop windows went along to have a good night out. Nutters often tag along with football crowds just for the buzz.

I have had many good days out watching Chelsea and have made many good friends who became my travelling companions to England games. Steve Jones loved Chelsea and, more importantly, he loved the thrill of the terraces. Football, I don't think he understood. He just knew that you cheered loudly when Chelsea scored and that you went in the opposition's end and punched people in the head for fun; he also understood that it was necessary to invade the pitch from time to time. But you could never hold a conversation with him about the game itself. He came into the pub one night and spoke for forty minutes about a game he had attended without once mentioning the match. I don't think he ever watched football. He was one of those so-called supporters, found in every club, who spend the entire match watching the police and opposing fans, chanting obscenities at both.

Steve was also a bit of a ladies' man and at one time he was courting a vicar's daughter. She was desperate to attend a football match so he took her to a game down at Fulham, promising the vicar he would look after her. Halfway through the second half Chelsea invaded the pitch and he kissed her on the cheek and joined the invasion, leaving her to make her own way home! The vicar, wise man, decided that his daughter would be better off not seeing him again. When Steve went round to the vicarage the vicar, being a man of God, said to Steve, 'All football hooligans should be

hung up by the goolies. Now clear off, because you won't be
seeing my daughter again!'

Chelsea were playing away at Bolton and this was the big
crunch match for they were both slugging it out for promo-
tion. Chelsea fans, though, wanted to put on a real show for
the northern idiots. They have always organised themselves
well and were one of the first terrace firms to do so. On this
day the main faces organised it so that two of them were on
each train going to Bolton. They walked up and down the
trains giving this message: 'Today is the day that we hit the
Bolton end. Go into their end. If you get turned away at the
gate walk around the ground and try again.'

It worked well: loads got in. At about 2.45 a roar went up
and Chelsea charged. It was pandemonium. Kyle and Jacko
were just going in. A window opened and a red-faced chap
in his late fifties stuck his head out of the window and
shouted in a broad Lancashire accent, 'There's a bloody riot
in here!' He then shut the window. Kyle said it was pure theatre. Everybody outside burst out laughing. Why he had
opened the window Kyle never knew, and who he was talking to no one could work out, but he had just felt an urge to
tell everyone all about it.

Chelsea had been relegated and had one last away game
at Aston Villa – one last chance to show the First Division
what they would be missing and what the Second Division
had coming to them. The word was out at the Bridge. Villa's
popular end was the Holte end, and Chelsea had decided to
take it. The Holte end is a huge terrace, one of the best and
biggest covered ends in the First Division. Chelsea got in
there and generally mingled with the Villa fans. The roar
went up and the Villa fans scattered. The whole end
retreated across the terrace; it was a stunning sight. What
makes people run I will never know, but when a terrace does
run it is very impressive. It reminds you of one of those

wildlife films about Africa when herds of gazelles run from cheetahs. I remember another occasion at Chelsea when three young bobbies were standing on the gate at the entrance for away fans, and one of them obviously knew about football and was asking the fans who was the left-back for the team that Chelsea were playing. Any hesitation on the part of the fan and they would get turned away. It worked very well. The guy in front of me went up to the gate. The policeman looked at him.

'Who's Luton's left-back?' he asked.

The fan looked at him.

'Pass, Mr Magnusson, next question please.'

'Clear off, you cheeky bastard,' the policeman replied.

I laughed, and got turned away as well.

For the next home game, in the public houses around the ground frequented by the home fans, the programme was studied and all the fans who wanted to infiltrate the away supporters' end learned the names of the opposing players. The poor coppers on the gate never got a wrong answer all day, and the idea was abandoned soon afterwards.

When Chelsea dropped into the Second Division and Millwall were promoted from the Third into the Second, the clash of the hooligans was set up. I did not attend the match at Millwall (I had a wedding to go to) but decided I had to go to the Chelsea *versus* Millwall game at Stamford Bridge. Silly Vince and I attended together and entered the Shed end. This was where the action would be, for certain. We stood just off the centre of the terraces. There was a funny atmosphere in the Shed. Chelsea knew Millwall would come in but were not sure how and when. In fact they came in in small groups and waited for a fight to break out so that they could all group together. Vince and I had come to watch the action, but the expected fight broke out right where we were standing. Vince got punched in the mouth by a Millwall fan during the fracas and while lying on the ground got kicked

a few times. All the Chelsea fans backed off and stood petrified as the Millwall fans walked across the terraces towards
them. One Millwall fan took great delight in walking up to
the Chelsea fans who were backed up against the barrier
and could not run anywhere, and asking, 'Are you Chelsea?'

'No.'

Wallop, he punched one.

'Don't tell lies.'

And so on to the next one.

'Are you Chelsea?'

'Yes.'

Wallop. 'I hate Chelsea!'

Funny when you think back on it, but not so funny for
the poor guys getting hit.

Fighting had also broken out on the terrace below us and
the police had moved in. The Millwall fans at the other end
had pushed over a fence and it looked like a pitch invasion
was about to happen. Suddenly the Chelsea surged back at
the Millwall. I had just got Vince to his feet, and he was
slightly shaken up. A Chelsea fan who was convinced I was
Millwall punched me in the side of the head.

'You Millwall?' he asked.

'No, I'm not,' I replied.

'Sorry about the punch.'

He then charged down the terrace and into the Millwall
who were beating a hasty retreat down the terrace. Chelsea,
who had the numbers, surged down at the Millwall. The
police herded the Millwall on to the running track which
surrounds Chelsea and took them up to the other end, and
everyone stayed put till full-time. Chelsea were jubilant;
they had inflicted a defeat on Millwall. Basically, though, it
was no more than a bloody nose. The Millwall knew that the
real battle was to be fought in the streets outside. After the
game Vince and I hung around. The Chelsea knew the score
and drifted away into the cool night air. The Millwall waited

for a while and then started for home. They were standing in the road outside the Britannia pub. No Chelsea fans ventured down that road. It's one thing defending your end against attack, but it is quite another mixing it on the streets against Millwall.

Years later, Chelsea played Millwall at Stamford Bridge in the FA Cup. Millwall didn't come in the Shed this time but went into the East Stand. Millwall won three–two and after the game the Chelsea supporters waited in the quadrant outside the Shed. But they were waiting only because they felt they had to. No one wanted to wait near the front. The Millwall had been clever; they had waited in the ground until the crowds had gone. They knew the guys waiting for them would be the Chelsea elite. Out marched the Millwall and waded straight into the Chelsea, who backed off. Well, that is the politest way to put it. There were too many police for any extended action. Further down the road there was another clash between fans outside the Gunter Arms pub, in which the Chelsea fared slightly better. Millwall had brought nearly 5,000 fans to this match. In the next round they played Luton and at this game were the scenes that appeared on television which shocked the Prime Minister, Mrs Thatcher.

When a few years ago the strict segregation policy was introduced, the police took to locking in away fans so as to have time to clear the streets of home fans. It always makes me laugh at Chelsea to see the number of people who wait around posing, trying to look tough as if they are waiting to tear the opposing supporters limb from limb when they know perfectly well they will be moved on by the police. The advent of greater police organisation has given the poseurs even more room for manoeuvre.

One good day out at Chelsea was on the last game of the season. Chelsea had been promoted from the Second Division and had to play Hull. It was to be a celebration. The gates to the Shed were locked well before kick-off so I went on to the open terrace and stood near the front. I was attending the match with my friends Jacko and Leggy. Chelsea had decided to do a lap of honour before the game to thank the fans for a season of marvellous support. Out trotted the team, and a few fans decided to run round with them. The fences which had been knocked down by Millwall were still down at the open end. I fancied a lap of honour myself, so I ran round the pitch with the team. When the team stopped in front of the Shed and waved, I stood alongside them and waved as well. All the guys from Leatherhead who supported Chelsea were green with envy – an Arsenal fan doing a lap of honour with the Chelsea team!

In the first half of the match Chelsea scored, and there was another pitch invasion. They scored a second goal after half-time and this time it was a huge invasion. It seemed the whole open end wanted to slap the players on the back. A minute later another goal, and everyone charged on again. The poor police just gave up. Leggy, who was very overweight, decided that he had done enough jumping up from the terraces and running on to the pitch and back. He was so exhausted and short of breath that he got to the edge of the pitch and sat down next to the posse of press photographers. If Chelsea scored again, he was going to be the first on the pitch to congratulate the players. He held up his hands in front of his face, pretending he had a camera. The trouble is that Leggy is a funny-looking bloke and he couldn't resist constantly turning round and looking at the crowd with a silly grin on his face. By now everyone in the crowd was laughing. The policeman in front of us, who was facing the crowd, kept turning round to see what everyone was laughing at. He was getting most annoyed because he thought they were laughing at him. Then he turned round just as Leggy was making yet another face. Even the policeman managed a smile at this fat fellow taking photos with an imaginary camera.

'Get back over here,' yelled the policeman.

Just as Leggy was walking back looking rather sheepish and sure to get ejected from the ground, Chelsea scored a fourth goal and in the confusion of the invasion Leggy slipped back on to the terraces. Another fan later tried the Leggy trick with the photographers, but only succeeded in getting a clip round the ear for his trouble.

Football was always a working class pastime and this was reflected in the dress code. Flat caps and working clothes gave way to the uniform of the early seventies: donkey jackets and denim, with compulsory industrial footwear – the famous Doc Marten boot. In the late seventies the dress code changed again. The designer look set in; Armani, Pringle, Tachini and Lacoste became the hooligan's uniform. Dressed up it was easier to avoid the police, and to get served in pubs. With the massive police presence at some matches the poseurs had free rein to dress up to the nines and pretend they had courage – a bunch of latter-day Tall Erics. I wonder how these guys would have fared ten years earlier.

Sometimes two designer dressers would team up to form a designer duo, and one day this happened in Manchester's Arndale Centre. A duo were walking past a pub frequented by Manchester City fans. A group drinking outside wolf-whistled the two Chelsea fans. One of the Chelsea fans stopped.

'What are you divs whistling at? I'll give you something to look at.'

With that he dropped his jeans to reveal a pair of Tachini shorts being worn as underpants. He patted them and pointed at the logo.

'See boys, Tachini! One day you'll be wearing these – when you learn about fashion, that is.'

With that he pulled up his trousers, leaving the Mancunians staring open-mouthed.

I went into a pub once with a huge group of Chelsea fans and everyone settled down for a pre-match drink. The booze flowed and there was a disco in the pub. The disc jockey kept asking for music requests. It was the time of punk music, but the DJ wisely decided not to play such aggressive music as it might excite everyone. It got near closing time and the DJ decided he would risk one punk record, so he put on the Sex Pistols. It was not a clever move. Everyone went crazy, jumping up and down like madmen. A huge fight erupted in the pub and it was demolished. The poor DJ had his equipment wrecked by a guy being thrown across the disco.

On another occasion Chelsea were playing Newcastle away and as usual thousands of Chelsea fans made the trek north. The Geordies hated Chelsea even more than they hated wearing the latest fashions. Kev Taylor was a typical fan, circa 1982, walking around with designer labels and dripping with gold jewellery, compulsory gold belcher chain around his neck. He stood up against the fence separating the Cockneys from the Geordies.

'What's it like to have no job?' he chanted.

A policeman spotted him and ejected him from the ground. He knew Kev would be in trouble outside the ground, and said to him, 'You wait till the locals spot you. They'll eat you for dinner, you overdressed poof.'

Sure enough, he was immediately spotted outside the ground and was chased all around the town for about half an hour. Somehow he escaped, but he never wore his designer fatigues to an away match again.

Arsenal had played in the morning so in the afternoon Vince and I decided to go down to The Valley to see Charlton play Chelsea. Chelsea took thousands down to The

Valley, which was a sprawling concrete bowl. Sadly, it is now no more. The Chelsea fans took up residence in the covered end and drove out the Charlton fans. Charlton trounced Chelsea four–nil and the Chelsea fans went berserk, smashing up the ground and causing a great deal of damage around it. One funny incident that made me laugh happened during play. Chelsea were three–nil down but attacking. The ball went in the crowd and someone kept it, and the referee ordered another ball to be sent out. A minute later Chelsea attacked down the left. As the ball came over, the fan who had nicked the ball threw it on to the pitch, so there were now two balls. Chelsea immediately scored but the referee disallowed the goal because of the other ball being in the area. The Chelsea fans went mad and ripped down the wooden boarding at the front of the stand. The next thing I saw was Steve Jones hanging out of the stand with a fifteen-foot lump of wood ripped from the advertising hoarding, trying to bash the Charlton keeper on the head. I had lost Vince and was standing next to a Charlton supporter.

'Look at that nutter,' he said.

'I know him, he lives near me,' I replied.

'Well, I don't know where you come from, mate, but if that's the sort of idiot that lives down your way I suggest you move!'

I had to agree. After the game I was standing on the platform when I saw a policeman taking Vince away. As he walked past me I spoke to him.

'What for, Vince?'

'This guy's a pillock,' he replied.

It transpired that the police had been pushing everyone into a car park and a young kid had been crushed. Vince had shouted at the policeman, 'Stop pushing, you moron.'

'What did you say?' asked the policeman.

'Stop pushing, you moron.'

The policeman arrested Vince and he was charged with

using threatening words and behaviour. The next day he pleaded not guilty and was bailed.

The damage caused after the match by the Chelsea fans was substantial, and the following day questions were asked in the House of Commons. The next night's London *Evening Standard* had the details on the front page. Out of nine arrested, eight had pleaded guilty and been fined no more than fifty pounds. The only one to plead not guilty was Vince. The politicians were horrified. 'Jail These Thugs' screamed the headlines, and as Vince was the only one who had pleaded not guilty he thought he would cop the lot. When it finally came to court the policeman got up and came out with the biggest load of garbage I have ever heard in my life.

'I saw the accused shout, "There's the fucking Charlton, let's get them,"' is an example of the things he said.

Vince was shocked but had four good witnesses and was found not guilty, although he ended up over £250 out of pocket because he was refused costs. It's a poor man's justice when you win your case but end up losing money.

Vince's case highlighted the fear of many football fans, that of arbitrary arrest. I for one was much more frightened of arrest than I ever was of violence from rival fans – and I think I represented the consensus – especially when the law was changed to allow magistrates to inflict huge fines on convicted fans. The police were, like rival fans, seen as adversaries, someone to pit wits against and outmanoeuvre. You can't be a football fan and not have an opinion about the police, because everywhere one goes they are present in varying numbers and degrees of nastiness. Like most football fans I kept clear of direct confrontation with the boys in blue at football, and also gave a wide berth to policewomen, who seem to have something to prove to their male colleagues. The huge numbers of police deployed at football matches now make them slightly arrogant. It contrasts sharply to the early days when a lone bobby confronted by large warring factions was seen to be petrified.

Like all football fans I never missed a chance to laugh at the stupidity and idiosyncratic behaviour that the police often displayed. The trick was knowing when to laugh.

I spent many enjoyable days out at Chelsea, but for a variety of reasons I don't venture down there any more. But I retain fond memories of the big open terrace.

6

England Away

I love my country, as do all the travelling football fans, but I can find no excuse for the excesses of some England supporters. A lot of them feel they are on a nationalistic crusade and when they cross the Channel they must tell everyone 'We won the war', and 'Englishmen are superior'. Most travelling England fans also refuse even to try to speak the language of the country they're in, which tends to make us all appear ignorant. I don't know whether it is because we are an island race or because English history books are very often biased about our war contribution, but I have lost count of the number of times I have sat in a bar and heard the comment, 'We bailed these wankers out in the war'. I used to try to argue the point, but now I just sit back and listen.

It is difficult to trace the craze for following England to away matches, but it seems to be all the rage to get a Union Jack, put your club team's name on it and drape it around the ground so that people back home will see it on TV. What most of the fans do not even realise is that the true flag of England is the flag of St George.

English fans were involved in violent incidents all over Europe during the 1970s. The first time I became aware of large groups of supporters travelling and causing trouble was when England played in Copenhagen in 1978. A Spurs fan I knew came into a local pub on his return and talked about it all night. He raved on and on, and I believed him because he really was a rather boring guy and couldn't have made up a story that interesting. He told me that all the fans settled long-standing differences during the England game. I found out later that this was true to an extent.

Normally the largest group at England games abroad were Chelsea fans, and they didn't want to fight other England supporters. If you supported England then you were welcome to join them, and frequently other fans did. Chelsea also numbered among them a charismatic fellow who went to all the overseas England games. His name was Steven Hickmott, and everyone called him 'Hickey'. He was a real leader who stood out from the crowd. He had an outrageous hairstyle – a sort of flat-top but shorter – and would wear the same King Kurt T-shirt and patched jeans all the time. He was over six feet tall and talked in a loud, droning voice. I became good friends with him, and I also met another Chelsea fan, Terence Last, both men now doing ten years on football-related charges.

The West Ham fans, I found out, would never mix it with Chelsea unless they had the numbers, but would remain aloof and apart, as also did the Scousers, who used the England trips as an excuse for a bit of thieving. As well as these there were always groups of fans who went to the game who you would recognise at subsequent away trips. One such group was the Blackburn group of about ten; they were funny fellows, full of Lancashire wit. There were also travelling nutters you could spot a mile off. They travelled alone and linked up with other nutters to become the 'dynamic duos', and once you spotted them it was best to avoid them.

Then again there were loonies, the subtle difference between them and nutters being that while a nutter usually liked to fight or pick fights whatever the odds, a loony just did crazy things which could sometimes lead to fights. I much preferred loonies abroad because basically that is how foreigners see us anyway – slightly mad! Loonies would occasionally link up with nutters, however, and if I spotted that mixture I would leave the country!

The whole kaleidoscope of the terraces links together to travel to England games. Twenty years ago travelling Englishmen were welcome wherever they went; they brought wit, humour – and money. But today an England match usually means the full mobilisation of the police force, with the cancellation of leave for officers. I have seen the travelling English army and I'm sometimes quite ashamed to be of the same nationality. It is one thing having a punch-up in your own country, but quite another when it happens abroad.

England qualified for the European Championship finals in Italy in 1980 and a lot of England fans made their way out to see their first game against Belgium in Turin. As soon as the England fans got to the city, trouble started. Every night there were fights in the bars and confrontation with young Italians on the streets. I had already been to Turin when Arsenal had played there, so I knew that the Italians take their football seriously. In the match against Belgium England scored first, but when Belgium equalised the Italians in the crowd started cheering. Fighting broke out and the Italian police fired tear gas which affected the players.

In the next match, against Italy, feelings of hostility towards England were intense. The riot police allowed the Italians to spit all over the English fans while they turned a blind eye, but if you retaliated you were in trouble. The Englishman abroad had always been admired for his cool and reserve, but the biased crowd control that night would have needled a saint. The last game was in Naples – a rough city at the best of times – and England fans again had a rough ride.

After the European Championships England set about the task of qualifying for the World Cup, to be held in Spain. It seemed there should be no problem, as we were drawn in a group with Hungary, Romania, Switzerland and Norway. Bucharest, the capital of Romania, was widely regarded by football fans as the most boring city in the world, so the game that promised the best fun was the one to be played in Switzerland. Therefore a large contingent of England fans duly headed there, mostly by rail. When everyone had checked in at their hotels, they headed out on the town. The word out in the bars was that an Englishman had been stabbed by an Italian the previous night. Switzerland has a large Italian population, and it is well known that there is no love lost between English and Italian football fans, so every-body arranged to meet up that night to go out and hunt down the Italians. There was trouble that night, and the next day there were further disturbances at the game, which England lost two–one.

Four days later England beat Hungary three–one and put themselves back in contention. We only had to beat Norway to be certain of qualifying – but we lost. I was sitting at the bar in Miami Airport when I heard the result. I couldn't believe it. The World Cup in Spain would not happen for me. A Swedish guy came up to me and said, 'It is England's destiny not to qualify again for the World Cup.' Fortunately he was wrong and qualify we did, albeit through the back door, and I arranged to make the trip to Spain with Keith Chitty, my friend of many years.

The World Cup in Spain came at the right time for me. I was coming up to twenty-six so it would be my last trip on young people's half-price rail travel. When England qualified a lot of people said they would go to Spain, but like most statements made on the spur of the moment it had to be taken with a pinch of salt. But Keith, I knew, was a certain runner. The press made a big thing about how the England fans would cause trouble. But football fans are not stupid; everyone knew the reputation of the Spanish police, and who wants to spend time in a Spanish jail?

Bilbao was the venue for England's first three matches, and while it wasn't the most glamorous place, I was glad because of another event that was taking place at this time: the Falklands War. Most Spaniards did not agree with our going to war with Argentina, a Spanish-speaking country, but Bilbao is in the heart of the Basque country where the population do not consider themselves Spanish. I felt sure we would get a warm welcome as many Englishmen had fought against Franco alongside the Basques during the Spanish Civil War, and this did indeed prove to be the case.

The time arrived and Keith and I set off for Victoria to catch the first boat train to Paris; then on to Spain and the World Cup. This event takes place every four years, and in 1982 England were fancied by many to be in with a real chance of winning. England were due to play France in their first group match; Keith and I had no tickets, but I felt sure we would be able to buy them easily enough. The only problem was that Bilbao was very near the French border, so I thought that a lot of Frenchmen would be travelling to the game. The English FA had made no attempt to obtain tickets for travelling fans, possibly hoping they would not travel.

Nevertheless there were quite a few England fans on the train, although most only exchanged a few words. It was once on board the ferry that the party really started. Everybody gravitated towards the front bar and within twenty minutes or so a party atmosphere prevailed, with flags being hung up all round the bar. Keith and I tagged along with a group of guys from Oldham. One of them was called Dave and he had a funny gravelly voice, so 'Gravel Voice' became his nickname. He had a big beer belly which hung over a pair of Union Jack shorts, and he knew lots of silly songs. An American serviceman was drinking on his own and he came and joined us, although the following day I'm sure he wished he hadn't. Another chap also sat with us, but he didn't join in much. He wore a Charlton 'Pride of London' sweatshirt, and had a scar on his left cheek which made his mouth turn up one side so that it looked as if he was always smiling. I nicknamed him 'Smiler', and it stuck. Smiler looked like a nutter and he made me nervous.

Just before the boat docked, everyone got stocked up for the train journey to Paris with beer and duty frees. The journey turned into one big beano, with singing and dancing all the way. The French people on the train were amused by our antics, which were typical eccentric English fun. Everyone had to do a party piece. Smiler just sat and watched. The American serviceman was really drunk and decided he was coming to Bilbao with us. The train arrived in Paris and everyone took the Metro to the station with the link to Hendaye and the border with Spain. Once we got to the station we decided to store our luggage in lockers so we wouldn't have to carry it around. Smiler stashed his stuff, walked out of the station and walked up to a Frenchman and said, '*Français, monsieur?*'

'*Oui.*'

Crash! He hit the Frenchman and knocked him straight to the ground. He turned round and walked over to me.

'I hate Froggies,' he said.

I looked at Keith and said, 'We've got to lose him, fast.'

The American serviceman, who was all over the show by now, suddenly realised that he had no luggage: he had left it all on the train. He had also left behind a very expensive camera.

'How am I going to get back to the train station, guys?'

'Don't worry, Ginger knows the way,' everyone replied.

I offered to take him, and told Keith I would meet him back at the station at 11.00 p.m. because the train left at 11.30. The American was legless. He even bet me he could run across the track and back again. I didn't believe he would do it, but he did. 'I love you Brits, you're crazy!' he said. Somehow we made it back to the main station and we went to the left luggage office. The Frenchman on duty explained that the guy would have to return in the morning to see if his luggage had been returned, so the poor American left to spend the night in the US Embassy.

I made my way back to try to find Keith. I looked in a few bars, but couldn't find anyone. As I went into one restaurant, my worst nightmares were standing before me. Smiler was at the pay counter with a drunken Englishman I hadn't seen earlier. A 'dynamic duo' was on the loose. Smiler had put all his change on the counter and was shouting at the poor cashier, who was saying to him in French that they didn't accept English money.

'Listen, Froggie, it's proper money,' he yelled, and he banged on the counter.

About six Frenchmen were sitting on stools near the door at the bar. I tried to beat a hasty retreat, but Smiler spotted me.

'Ginger, come here and tell her about proper money.'

The Frenchman at the bar said something.

'Wanna mix it, Froggie?' shouted Smiler.

I could see an international incident developing and the three of us ending up in prison. The drunk with Smiler, who was from Manchester, uttered some words of wisdom: 'Let's do a runner.' Unfortunately the guy could hardly walk, let alone run. I decided to save the day, and walked up to the pay counter.

'*Excusez-moi, mademoiselle. Combien coûte l'addition, s'il vous plaît?*'

'C'est cinquante francs, monsieur, s'il vous plait.'

I gave her a 500-franc note. She gave me the change and I put it in my pocket along with Smiler's 'proper' money. I walked Smiler and the drunken Mancunian to the door, but as the latter walked past the six Frenchmen he uttered the dreaded phrase you hear from drunken Englishmen in France: 'We bailed you tossers out in the war.'

'I think they want a row, Ginger,' said Smiler.

'No they don't. Let's get out of here,' I replied.

I got them out of the door and said I would meet them later in a bar down the road but that I had to eat first. When they got round the corner I shot off in the opposite direction. Thank God I'll never see them again, I thought.

I got back to the station, where we were due to catch the 11.30 train, at about ten past eleven. Gravel Voice and his mates were there, but no Keith.

'Where's Keith?' I asked.

'I don't know. He disappeared shortly after you left and we haven't seen him since.'

They took their gear out of the lockers and went for the train. I waited, and as it got closer to the time of the train's departure I cursed Keith. He finally turned up at one in the morning.

'Where the hell have you been?'

'I met up with some mad Portsmouth fans and we had a punch-up in a bar, so I had to go for a drink with them.'

I was livid, but I burst out laughing when Keith couldn't remember where he had put some of his gear. He accused the Oldham guys of having nicked it, but the truth was that he had forgotten where he'd put it. He had lost his cassette player, cassettes, England flag, scarves and a camera.

We eventually left for Spain on the 2 a.m. train. The next morning when we arrived both of us looked and felt terrible. We crossed the border and looked for a train to San Sebastian, and while we waited we went into a bar near the station. As mentioned earlier, bars are great places to get information. I met some guys who had been staying in Biarritz and they told me everyone had headed into Bilbao to buy match tickets as they were in very short supply; the Spanish had loads and were ripping off the English.

We boarded the train and as I got on I saw the front page of the Spanish newspaper: 'GENERAL MENENDEZ ACCEPTE LA RENDITION.' We all knew what this meant. The Falklands War was over, and Britain had won. I thought that would probably make the Spaniards a little bit antagonistic towards us.

Once in San Sebastian we found out that everyone was indeed going to Bilbao because tickets were hard to come by, so we went along to the bus station and bought our tickets. The bus was due in half an hour so we found a bar and went in. Inside we saw a big skinhead wearing a Bulldog Bobby T-shirt (England's official team mascot). On his arm was a Union Jack tattoo.

'All right, mate?' I asked.

'Ja, I am fine,' he answered.

I was flabbergasted. He was German, although he was dressed in England colours and had a British tattoo. He continued, 'I must drink twenty-five lagers before I am a proper Englishman.' I would have burst out laughing, but he looked pretty tough. I learned from a couple of other people in the bar that three Londoners had met him there and told him that he had to have certain credentials before he could even contemplate becoming an English football fan. One was that he had to like punching Froggies; two, he had to like going to the toilet in public; and three, he had to be able to drink twenty-five lagers. I couldn't believe it, but this guy was sticking to his task manfully. Keith and I left him to it and caught the bus to Bilbao.

Sitting on the bus I had a good laugh to myself about the German. Why on earth would a German want to become an English football fan? I suppose it must have been because the youth of other nations saw us in a romantic light. English football fans were a tough, sometimes outrageous group of people having an exciting time and cocking a snook at everybody. The established order couldn't stop them, and that was part of the mystique of being an England fan. The German obviously felt that there were some sort of initiation tests that he had to complete in order to become part of the gang. If only he had realised that by just turning up he had already become an England fan. I am sure that his cause was not helped by everybody goading him on.

We arrived in Bilbao and decided to leave our gear in left-luggage lockers, but there weren't any at the station – they had been removed because of the threat of terrorist explosives. We found a hotel in the cheap part of town. The street was narrow and because of this the sun never shone on it, so consequently it was always cool. We dumped our gear and went back on the streets looking for information. We found out that tickets had been sold at the bullring the previous day and a rumour was going around that it would open again at five that evening for all the England fans to get tickets. That gave us two hours to walk up there. We set off up the road and saw a load of England fans outside a little window. On the window were pictures of hamburgers, sausages and chips with a list of prices. Outside were beer barrels and England fans eating hamburgers and chips to their hearts content. The windows were steamed up.

'All right, lads?' asked a northern voice.

'Yeah, okay,' we replied.

'Cockneys, eh?'

'Yeah.'

'Who's your team, pal?'

'Arsenal, but he's Newcastle,' I said, pointing to Keith. This was the ritual conversation when rival club fans met at England games.

So for the first time I came upon 'Greasy Joe's Hamburger

Joint', as it was generally known. It became the focal point for England fans, who lived on a staple diet of chips and beer. Greasy Joe's was about fifty yards from the railway station, and everyone who went to Bilbao knew it. You walked in and were instantly hit by a wall of heat. Inside was a little counter and behind it was an overweight Spaniard cooking for his life. Sweat poured off him and grease and grime were thick on the walls. The owner would open up and start cooking at 7 a.m. and still be going at 2 a.m. the next morning. He was extremely fast; you would order the meal of your choice and he would cook it on the spot. Once you had eaten he would shout out 'Pay!' and you went up and told him what you'd had. In between he would also pour beer. It would have been easy to walk out without paying, but I don't think many did. He was earning a fortune, and as far as he was concerned English football fans were the greatest. There was only enough room for stools around the walls and little shelves were put up for the plates. I never went past there without seeing it bursting at the seams with people stuffing their faces. The night before the France game the owner locked the doors and let ten England fans sleep on the floor, giving them a bottle of Bacardi to drink as a nightcap.

Keith and I made our way along the narrow unevenly paved streets which led to the bullring. Keith suggested a bite to eat and I saw a restaurant that looked cheap and cheerful. It was a cafeteria-style oval bar with big stools positioned round the counter area. We sat one side, and on the other was a good-looking guy with an England Bulldog Bobby T-shirt.

When he spoke it became obvious he hailed from the Bristol area. Sitting next to him was a gorgeous-looking girl and the guy was revelling in the attention and looks she was receiving.

'All right, lads, what do you think?' he asked.

'Lovely,' I replied.

'I met her in Paris and she decided she wanted to come to Bilbao with me.'

It transpired that she was Swedish and hardly spoke a word of English, but they seemed to be communicating with each other okay. I was more interested in getting tickets for the football than listening to his stories about how they had met.

'Have you got any tickets for the France game?' I asked.

'No,' he replied with an uncaring shrug of his shoulders. 'You going?'

He smiled. 'Depends if I get out of bed.'

'You big-headed bastard!' Keith replied.

The guy from Bristol got up and left with the girl, obviously realising that Keith had taken a dislike to him. 'I'm glad he left, because I think I might have smacked him in the head,' said Keith.

We left the restaurant and climbed a steep hill, and as we came over the brow we were confronted by an explosion of colour. A huge, dusty open space in front of the red-brick-walled bullring was filled with about five hundred England fans covered in Union Jack and St George flags, hats, scarves and T-shirts: a human collage of red, white and blue. There were six pay windows, boarded up with railings directly in front for people to queue in between, and lots of guys were sitting on the railings or standing directly in front of the windows, making sure they would be first to get tickets when the windows opened. Others, such as Keith and myself, walked around the area just mingling and listening to all the latest stories. Keith struck up conversation with a group of Geordies who, even though it was quite warm, were wearing woollen scarves. One of them was covered in bruises and scratches.

'Christ, you've had a beating, mate,' I said.

'No, I fell off the roof of a train,' he replied.

I burst out laughing. 'What were you doing up there?'

One of his mates told us the full story as the guy himself was a bit embarrassed by our laughter. They had been to Biarritz and his mate had lost all his money playing blackjack in the casino. He had enough to get to Bilbao where he was going to get some more wired out to the bank, but on the rickety train from San Sebastian he had had a great money-making idea. Unfortunately the inspiration had come to him after a lot of alcohol had been consumed. 'Right, lads,' he had announced, 'I'm gonna get up on the roof of the train and sing "The Blaydon Races". Who wants to bet five hundred pesetas I can't do it?' There was no shortage of people in the train carriage who wanted to put their money into a hat which was passed round. He stripped off down to his shorts and clambered out of the window. Normally he would have managed it, but under the influence of drink it didn't look good. No sooner had he stood on the roof than he fell off. Someone pulled the communication cord and as the train screeched to a halt everyone ran back down the track, fearful for the Geordie's welfare. He emerged from the bushes at the side of the track, bruised and shaken but otherwise unhurt. The first words he uttered were, 'No refunds, lads.' The poor Spanish railway guard could not make it all out, and neither could the other passengers.

Keith and I roared with laughter. I have noticed on my England travels that the Geordies all seem to be big drinkers. I have never come across any other group of fans who could outdrink them. In fact, later in Spain I was to see a stupid Chelsea fan try; he ended up totally legless, while the Geordies were still sober.

A huge roar went up from the crowd. I thought the ticket office had opened, but I looked round to see a huge skinhead and his friend walking down the hill towards the bullring holding bottles of red wine above their heads, at the same time chanting 'England!' They were both very drunk and it

was impossible to get any sense out of them. The skinhead
was wearing a green US flying jacket unzipped to the waist,
was shirtless and had a Union Jack tattooed on his chest.
They lurched around the open area, chanting 'England, we
love you' several times, then staggered off down the hill
together arm in arm, swigging from their wine bottles. After
they had gone someone told me that they had been walking
around blind drunk for three days. No one knew where they
came from because they didn't hang around long enough
for anyone to get a sober word out of them. The skinhead
had been pictured on the front page of a prominent Spanish
newspaper under the headline 'This is an England fan'. God
knows what the average Spaniard thought when they saw
him.

Five o'clock passed and the ticket offices didn't open as
expected. The friendly mood among the crowd began to
change. A couple of people banged on the wooden shutters.
'Come on, open up.' The general consensus was that any
trouble would be caused by our inability to obtain match
tickets. A few Spaniards appeared with fistfuls of tickets
which they were offering at vastly inflated prices. A few
people paid 3000 pesetas for a 300-peseta ticket, and a group
of Leeds fans walked around remonstrating with them for
buying the tickets.

'Don't buy off the slags. They're ripping us off.'

One of the Leeds fans pushed a Spanish tout in the chest.
'Clear off, you rip-off merchant.'

One of the others walked up to the tout. 'Sorry, mate,
how much are the tickets?'

'Three thousand pesetas, *señor*.'

'Let's have a look.'

The Spaniard showed him the tickets. The Leeds fan
looked at two of them closely, put them in his pocket and
walked five paces away to his friends. The Spaniard walked
after him, but was pushed in the chest.

'Walk away, Dago, or you'll get a slap.'

The Spaniard, seeing he was on a hiding to nothing, walked away. Other people seeing this did the same. A fat Northerner tried the same trick, but the Spaniard fancied his chances against the fat man, grabbed him round the neck and dragged him towards the crowd of Spaniards who gathered on the edge of the forecourt. The group of Leeds fans saw this and ran over, slapping the Spaniard round the head and making him let go and run for it. Just at that moment an Italian walked on to the forecourt with a box full of rosettes, unaware of the ugly mood among the England fans. He had walked only five steps when he was punched in the side of the head. He dropped his rosettes and ran off; someone picked up the box and threw it into the air, scattering the rosettes everywhere. 'Now clear off, you Dago bastards, and stop ripping off English people,' someone shouted.

The police turned up and walked across the forecourt, pursued by the Italian waving his arms wildly. The guy who had belted him disappeared, as did a few others. The Italian pointed out a few innocent people and the Spanish police started searching them for the stolen rosettes. A crowd gathered and insults and accusations flew – on one side the Italian and Spanish traders, on the other the England football fans. The senior Spanish policeman in the middle, who spoke English, announced his decision which was binding on all parties. The Italian was to get nothing; the Spaniards were to return to their shops; and the English were to leave the bullring forecourt since the ticket office would not be opening as all the tickets had been sold. A couple of people questioned the policeman about tickets, but with no luck. I walked back down the hill with Keith towards the town centre to cruise the bars to see if anyone had tickets or information. During our travels it seemed that about half of the people we met possessed tickets. I was beginning to feel a little worried, but we decided to have a drink and if forced we would snatch tickets from a tout as a last resort.

We settled down in a small bar, and later in the evening a group of England fans from Manchester came in and started talking to us. They had been in Bilbao for three days, and had an interesting story to tell. The previous evening everyone had gathered in a big restaurant-bar down by the river because of rumours that the local taxi drivers were selling tickets from the big taxi rank nearby. A couple of fans had bought tickets for well above face value, and the taxi drivers were waving wads of tickets and taunting the England fans who had formed into a big group outside the bar. One guy had walked across to the group of taxi drivers, snatched a few tickets and run back over to the England fans without paying. One of the drivers had then stepped forward and offered to fight any England fan. One fan had walked forward, pretending he didn't understand, and while the taxi driver was not expecting it had thumped him, knocking him to the ground. The other drivers had then run over to join in, and that had led to the England fans joining the fray. A knife had been flashed and one of the taxi drivers had ended up with stab wounds (rumour was that he had subsequently died). In the end the police had turned up and an England fan had been taken away.

We were all in total agreement that this had been the fault of the English FA. None of the trouble would have happened if people had been able to buy tickets.

Keith and I went from bar to bar talking to different people. In one place I heard three London fans telling an outrageous story to a group of northern fans. Londoners, Cockneys to all football fans not from London, see themselves as a superior bunch in terms of their dress sense, language (nicknaming ability and rhyming slang) and success with women. I think other groups of fans see Cockneys as simply flash. There is no doubt that Cockneys love their notoriety and the animosity they arouse in other fans. These three were all in their mid to late twenties and were well groomed, and they were drinking San Miguel lager from the bottle, although none of them seemed drunk. One appeared to be the spokesman and gestured with his face and hands when he talked. Sometimes when he used a phrase he put a deliberate drawl on the end of a word to give it more effect. 'We're the leaders of Millwall's F Troop and my pal is the famous "Harry the Dog",' he was saying. The Northerners were pretty impressed by the claims and stories of the three, especially the one about the scalping of the rival fan outside the Cold Blow Lane end. They left the bar chattering amongst themselves, in awe of the Cockneys' stories.

The Londoners then looked over at us. 'All right, lads?' one called out.

Keith and I walked over.

'You Cockneys?' one of them asked.

'Sort of, we're from Surrey,' I replied.

'Are you going to tell us a story then?' asked Keith.

'No, mate, we're only interested in stitching up northern divs (idiots). As far as we're concerned everyone who lives more than forty miles outside London must be told a story because living that far from the smoke they must be gullible.'

'Are you Millwall?' I asked.

'No we're Chelsea, but one of those fools came straight up and asked if we were Millwall, so we obliged them.'

I don't like to stereotype people, but many London football fans do tend to think of 'Northerners' (anyone from North of Watford) as people who wear flat caps, eat meat and potato pies and live in places like Coronation Street. And all western and East Anglian fans are perceived as farm workers.

The three Chelsea fans had been going around telling stories non-stop to anyone who would listen, and as they were such good raconteurs I felt sure they would have taken

in a lot of people. They were well dressed; all three were covered in designer label clothes.

'What are you dressed up for, a local nightclub or something?' Keith asked.

'Nah, we feel we have to show these people the correct
standards.'

'It's your Cockney panache and élan, innit?' one of the
others chipped in.

I meant to ask them their names but I was laughing so
much I completely forgot, although I doubt that I would
have got a truthful answer anyway. I mentioned the German
guy I had encountered in San Sebastian, and the three of
them burst out laughing.

'We couldn't believe our luck, mate. This Kraut
approached us and asked us how to become a proper
England fan.'

Apart from what the German had told me, they had
also told him he must learn how to say 'Kill the Bill' (beat
up the police) and 'The referee's a wanker' in a Cockney
accent. They had left him in San Sebastian in the bar
where we had seen him, only the day before. When I told
them of our meeting with him twenty-four hours later
they collapsed on the floor. Then they left, saying, 'No
disrespect, lads, but we've got to find someone else to
stitch up.' Other stories they had told were that Hickey
had bought a gun in Paris and was going to shoot the
leader of West Ham, and that people with Cockney accents
were getting sex at half price in the brothels in Bilbao
because the whores knew class and didn't expect
Cockneys to pay as much. I never saw them again, but I
was to hear more about them.

It was midnight in Bilbao and in seventeen hours' time
England would play France, yet Keith and I hadn't seen a
single Frenchman. We were determined to find one, and at
last we spotted three in a bar. There were a few other

England fans in there and as we walked in the French guys shook our hands warmly.

'*Bonjour messieurs*,' I said.

The three of them cheered. One of them said, '*Parlez-vous français, monsieur?*'

'*Un peu, un petit peu*,' I replied.

They roared with laughter and bought us some wine. We stayed drinking with them for two hours and had a real laugh, even though we didn't understand what they said and vice versa. It was only tiredness that eventually broke us up, and we retired to bed.

I was up the next morning at about nine. I felt terrible, but excited about the match. I woke Keith so that we could go in search of some match tickets. We went downstairs and into the street, where England fans were drinking and sitting on the pavement. I entered a little café and on top of the counter were small snacks, seafood and cold omelette on French bread. I helped myself, not realising they were not free. I came out with two beers and ordered an omelette for breakfast. Vanloads of riot police came up the road every five minutes and looked at us warily. We stared back at them. Two Geordies were sitting on the steps of a house, swigging from bottles of red wine. One of them passed a bottle to me, saying, 'Drink some of this, it's nice.' I drank, but it was like vinegar and my face creased up at the sour taste. The Geordies looked at me, wondering why I wasn't enjoying the wine.

'You must be Chelsea because they are all bairns and can't drink either,' they said.

'You must have metal-lined stomachs to drink this,' I replied.

They laughed, and we started talking. I always liked meeting Geordies at England games because they are so blunt and friendly.

Breakfast came and went and at about eleven I decided to

go and look for our mate Kyle in Greasy Joe's. We walked up
the cobbled street and into the sunlight. The heat immediately struck us. Everywhere we looked there were England
fans and riot police. The road we were on would take us up
to the San Mames stadium and every bar on the way would
be full of England fans. No sign of Kyle in Greasy Joe's, so I
thought a trip up to the bullring to look for tickets was
worth a try. Once at the bullring an old woman approached
us asking 2000 pesetas for 300-peseta tickets. I could have
taken them if I had wanted, but I resented the price.

We headed towards the ground. I began to think that no
French people were going to turn up. We went into a bar
and spoke to a few guys who had all bought tickets that
morning for 500 pesetas. It was so hot that Keith needed a
cool lager, so we stayed for a while. The bar started filling up
and most people seemed to be getting tickets somehow,
either purchasing them or snatching them. I still thought I
would get some later. Then a group of Frenchmen walked
into the bar. One of them pulled out a wad of pesetas and
shouted, 'Beer for the English!'

He brought everyone a beer, and also bought a bottle of
spirits and two little glasses and went round toasting everyone. He would give someone a glass and then have one
himself, pouring a little in each glass every time and pro-
posing a toast. 'Watch out, lads, he's probably a bummer,'
said one fan. But in fact there was no motive on his part
other than promoting friendship between English and
French fans. All the French fans I met that day were the
same. They wanted to shake your hand with the words, 'May
the best team win.'

By now, about one o'clock, the French were starting to
turn up in droves. Most of the England fans had taken up
residence in the bars in the square of streets behind the
ground. One particular bar on the corner was packed;
Hickey and the Chelsea fans had taken over the place. Down

the road as far as the eye could see were police vans full of
riot police. Over the road on the corner was the Winston
Churchill pub, but this was also very crowded. Keith and I
found a perfect bar on the main road and set up residence
with about thirty other England fans. We stood outside
asking about tickets, and everyone seemed to have one but
none to sell. I nevertheless felt confident that I would get
two for Keith and me. Coach after coach was coming down
the road packed with French fans, and they were all waving
at us. Nearly every Frenchman was wearing an 'Allez France'
hat and had their national colours displayed on a rosette.

Suddenly there was a shout. 'Ginger!' It was Kyle, walking
up the road. We greeted each other like long-lost brothers
and began talking excitedly. I found out that he was staying
in the same road as us, and that he had a match ticket. By
now the streets around the ground had taken on a carnival
atmosphere. A band marched past and I stopped them. They
were wearing white boiler-suit type clothing but I failed to
notice the letters SNCF on their breast pockets. SNCF stands
for Société Nationale des Chemins de Fer (the French railways), but I didn't realise it was a French band. 'Play us a
tune, lads,' I shouted. '"Rule Britannia" or "God Save the
Queen" will do.'

The band stopped in the slip road, which by now was full
of people, and struck up the music. I recognised it: the
French national anthem. Within thirty seconds the bar was
surrounded by French people singing and dancing, and this
went on for about ten minutes. The French completely took
over the corner and a Frenchman came round with a hat.

'What have you done, Ginger?' someone asked.

I was not finished yet, though, and stopped the band to
demand 'Rule Britannia'. They struck up again, this time
with a fast dance number. A Frenchman started dancing and
beckoned me forward. I joined him and shouted to Keith,
'Get round with the hat and get some beer money for us.' So

Keith went round and got plenty of money. He nodded at me and we retreated to a bar about fifty yards down the road. All the other England fans who had been in the bar on the corner had come down, and I got a warning: 'Don't stop another French band, or else!'

I bought beers with the money that Keith had collected and distributed them. By now everyone had seen the funny side of it and we were all laughing. The bar we were in was tiny and all the owner had was a small refrigerator full of beer. It became obvious that he was running out of beer fast. He shouted out something and an old man, who was obviously his father, appeared and was sent off across the main road through the lines of traffic. It was a dual carriageway and the police were doing their best to keep the coaches moving. A few minutes later the old man reappeared with a crate of San Miguel lagers on his head. He got back to the bar with our cheers ringing out, then off he went again. He must have been over seventy years old, but he came back again with another crate on his head, weaving in and out of the traffic. He set off for a third trip, but was so exhausted that he decided to give up and sat down on a chair. The bar was drunk dry, so we moved on. I suddenly realised that Keith and I had still not got tickets and it was only forty minutes from kick-off. I spotted a Spaniard with tickets and approached him.

'Tickets?'

'Si, señor.'

'What have you got?'

He pulled out two seat tickets which had a face value of 900 pesetas each.

'Very good seats,' he said.

'How much?'

'Eight thousand pesetas.'

'No. Too much.'

'Eight thousand pesetas,' he said again.

'Okay, show me.'

He passed them to me and I put them in my pocket. I pulled out my money and gave him four thousand pesetas. He looked at me and said, 'No, eight thousand pesetas.' He gave me my money back. I now had the tickets and the money. I could have run if I had wanted, but I said, 'Now listen here, I am giving you a good deal and you know it. Now take the money or else I will pay you face value only.'

He didn't understand English but knew I wouldn't budge, so he took the four thousand grudgingly. I walked back to Keith and Kyle. Keith was well pleased – best seats in the house for a tenner. The heat was now oppressive and I bought a bottle of water to drink at half-time. Kyle left us to go on to the terraces. The heat inside the stadium was so bad that Kyle was sick and passed out. An American photographer took some pictures of Kyle lying there, so I wonder if he was featured in an American magazine under the caption 'An English Football Fan'. Keith and I got to the gate and my water bottle was confiscated – or so I thought. At half-time the same guy who had confiscated the water returned it to me – he had put the bottle in a refrigerator.

Once inside the stadium I got paint all over my shoes from where they had been painting it that morning. The stadium was packed and Union Jacks and French flags adorned every available space, but the French must have outnumbered the English by two to one numerically. The teams came out and everyone cheered. Kick-off, and after twenty seconds England scored. Keith and I went berserk. The best seats were under cover in the shade, and we were the only two Englishmen in this stand. The French looked at us. France equalised but in the second half England scored two more goals. At the end of the game the French people around us shook our hands sportingly, saying '*Très bon*' and '*Bryan Robson magnifique*'.

The England fans were overjoyed and we all danced

down the street. The riot police didn't know what to make of it all. Keith, Kyle and I set up camp in a bar on the big main road that goes through the centre of Bilbao. There was a huge bar on the left-hand side of this street with a lot of tables outside, and we sat there watching everyone file past. A fantastic car came into view. It was an old Austin van which had been painted in the colours of the Union Jack. It had boards in the back for people to sit on and it was called 'The Iron Lady' – the well-known nickname of Prime Minister Maggie Thatcher. Everyone cheered at the car as it drove past, and the driver went down the street honking the old-style air horn on the side. I spotted Gravel Voice over the road in a bar, and went over for a chat with him and his friends. Keith also spotted him, and came over. Gravel Voice told us that they were all going down to the red-light district to celebrate England's great win.

'You coming with us, Ginger?'

'I don't know. I'll ask Keith.'

Keith walked across and punched Gravel Voice right in the face. 'You slag, you nicked my cassette.'

'No I didn't, I promise.'

'Well it wasn't in the locker when I got back.'

'We never touched your locker, mate, honest.'

I dragged Keith away and took him across the road. I thought he was being unreasonable and told him so. I went back over and spoke to Gravel Voice, who by now had a thick lip.

'Sorry about Keith.'

'No problem, Ginger. Are you coming with us?'

'No, I'll stick with Keith.'

They moved off. Keith, Kyle and I celebrated well into the small hours, and the next morning we decided to move out to San Sebastian. Everyone was moving out of Bilbao, but would be back in a few days for the next match. We crossed the bridge over the river. The water was badly polluted and was a mahogany brown colour. 'Nothing could live in that,' said Kyle.

San Sebastian is a lovely Spanish town, but we found it difficult to find accommodation there. We went into one apartment block but the woman there, who spoke good English, told us that she had had to throw out the last football fans to board there because they urinated in the lift, been sick everywhere and upset the other residents. I promised that we would redeem the name of England, and she relented. The room was spotless. That night we headed out on the town. San Sebastian is a real Spanish town, but the two places where the England fans drank were Club Hollywood and the place Keith and I took up residence, the Twickenham bar. Inside there is a rugby ball hanging down from the bar, hence its name. We walked in and I got talking to the owner. He was in his late thirties and looked fit and tanned. His wife helped him with the bar, and was very pretty. Another girl was sitting at the bar and the owner introduced her to me as his sister. She was also very pretty, about the same age as myself and had dark hair and eyes.

We settled in at the bar and the conversation went on into the night. I told the owner that my grandfather had fought in the International Brigade, and from that moment on I was made guest of honour. The owner explained to me that the Basques had a different language and flag to the rest of Spain, and that anyone who ordered a drink in the Basque language got a larger measure. The arguments and banter between the Cockneys and Northerners in the bar went on into the small hours, and much the worse for drink I organised a North *versus* South football match on the beach the next morning at ten. We staggered home very early in the morning and didn't even wake up until ten. We got down to the seafront at about 11.20 a.m. and I noticed the tide was in. Thank God for that. I felt terrible. As we walked along, a big roar went up.

'Oi, Cockney, is that your team?'

I looked over and standing outside a bar were about thirty Northerners chanting at us. 'Where were you at ten o'clock?' they sang.

'My boys checked out the tides and stayed in bed. We automatically assumed you lot would do the same,' I shouted back.

The jeers and catcalls rang out, and I felt stupid. I went down on to the beach and Hickey and a load of his pals were sitting around a giant stereo. They were talking about whether or not they would have a punch-up in Club Hollywood with the Scousers. One of the Scousers had stolen some money the night before from a Spanish girl's handbag and had created a lot of bad feeling. But most of the talk every day was about the next match and who we would play in the final. England were to meet Czechoslovakia in the next game, and we decided to go the day before and stay two nights in Bilbao so that we could easily get tickets. It should be a doddle to get tickets for this game anyway.

The next night we went back down to the Twickenham bar and the same crowd were in there; it was like a little drinking club. Two Manchester fans who had not been in before came in and sat at the bar. We sat talking with them, and I told them about Smiler and about how he frightened me, as well as all the other stories of incidents that had happened. Manchester people generally do not like Scousers, so they in turn told me stories about the Scousers' thieving in Paris.

At about midnight I felt a tap on my shoulder and I heard Keith whisper, 'Don't look round unless you have to.' I did turn, and standing there was Smiler. I was absolutely dumbstruck. Of all the people from England I didn't want to see, he was the one person I would have given my right arm to avoid. I felt the goose bumps on my neck rise and a feeling of uneasiness spread through my body. I tried to stay calm, and looked up as if I was pleased to see him.

'Hello, Ginger. I lost you in Paris.'

'Well, you've found me now. Want a drink?'

'Yeah, I'll have a lager.'

I ordered him a beer and he took it and went to sit down on his own, his usual position. His face held no expression. Most people in a similar situation would look for eye contact to start up a conversation, but not Smiler; looking into Smiler's eyes was like looking into a bottomless lake. I felt the need to make some conversation with him as I felt so uneasy, although I knew that it wouldn't work and he would stay on his own.

'Smiler, where's your mate from Manchester?' I asked.

'Who?' replied Smiler, as if the guy didn't exist.

'You know, the guy you were with in that restaurant.'

'I dunno, still in Paris I suppose.'

I laughed to myself at the irony of the situation. I couldn't believe he had found us again. Later in the evening he hit a Spaniard in the bar and then turned round and said to me, 'I hate Dagos.' I began to wonder if there was a nation on earth he didn't dislike. I must have looked concerned because he said, 'You know your trouble, Ginger, you worry too much.' I was certainly worried about him. I returned to the bar and the two Manchester guys said, 'I see what you mean. He worries us too.'

Smiler went and sat down on his own. I was glad about that. Occasionally I would glance round at him, but he just sat impassively with that sickly smile on his face. Any book written about body language certainly didn't apply to him. Later that evening he left the bar and I was never to see him again – or so I hoped. I swear that if England play in Timbuktu I will bump into him in a bar in the middle of nowhere. Many years later I was watching a report on the TV news of the last game played at The Valley, home of Charlton FC, and as the reporter was interviewing people who had been to the ground I looked more closely. People were gathered around the reporter, and at the back of the crowd I saw the face. I looked again and sure enough, there was Smiler standing in the background and not saying anything. I was expecting him to punch the TV crew and say the words 'I hate TV crews' – but he didn't. All I can say about that man is that I am glad he liked me. He was a complete nutter. Plenty of nutters follow England, but he was the craziest I ever met.

We headed back to Bilbao and once there we found a fabulous local restaurant overlooking the river in the old part of town. It was full of local people and the first time we ate in there they seemed honoured by our presence. The owner sent over a bottle of red wine for us to drink with our dinner. The food was excellent and we vowed to return the next night, which we duly did. This time the ugly side of football reared its head. We sat down at a table inside the restaurant. The governor was pleased to see us, and while we ate a hearty meal two Scousers came in and sat near the doors. Because of the climate of Spain the front was a big open area which was closed by pulling down shutters across the whole frontage. The two Scousers ate their food quickly, looking round nervously. I suspected something so I walked over to them.

'Don't do a runner, lads. It will look bad on us.'

'Okay,' they replied.

I went back and sat down again, but five minutes later they jumped up and ran. The Spanish people in the bar all looked at us. I don't speak Spanish, but I could tell what they were saying. The atmosphere in the restaurant changed completely. Keith and I finished our meal with people staring at us and quietly talking amongst themselves. I went up and paid as soon as possible, and we left. I never went into that restaurant again as I didn't feel we would be welcome.

The day of the game against Czechoslovakia arrived and everybody gathered in the streets down in our little district.

Lots of people had luggage with them and were heading back to various destinations as soon as the game was over. A few were bound for Madrid to buy tickets for the final, which they were convinced England would reach. As there were no left-luggage lockers in the station, everyone stored their gear in the back room of a little café we had taken over during our stay in Bilbao. The woman who ran it had really taken the England fans to heart. She charged about all the time, seeming to have the capacity to cook, serve beer and take money all at the same time.

That morning something happened which told us a lot about what the England fans would have to expect in Madrid. Because of the politics of the Basque region, a lot of policemen were brought in from Madrid. The police station in Bilbao was like a fortress to protect it from terrorist attack. A stocky guy called Dave, from Birmingham, came down the street and lifted his shirt. He had horrible weals and bruises all over his body. The police had picked him up the previous night and given him a fearful beating, apparently because England had won the Falklands War. The Spanish bar owner took him upstairs and cleaned him up. As she came back into the street a vanload of riot police drove past and she screamed abuse at them.

Later on that morning four guys came down the street and walked up to me.

'What's it like down here?' they asked.

Scousers, I thought to myself. 'It's okay, we're really popular,' I said.

'How much is it?'

'Really cheap.'

'Yeah, well we've been in Spain two weeks and none of us have got any money.'

'How are you coping?' I asked.

'Gibbing in, thieving, doing runners.'

'Yeah, well, don't do it around here because we're very

popular down here and we don't need you to mess it up,' I said.

They nodded acknowledgement and walked on. Two or three minutes later they emerged from the bar carrying two bottles of wine. They walked up the road slowly towards us and I heard one say, 'I think she saw us.' The woman emerged and shouted at them.

'I hope you haven't stolen those, because if you have I will do you,' I said moving forward to thump them.

They put the bottles down on the pavement and ran up the road. The woman owner came up the street, picked up the wine and walked over to me. She spoke Spanish but I got the gist of what she was saying. 'Why did you do this?' – meaning the English people. I apologised and vowed that I would never again let any Scousers thieve near me.

Keith and Kyle were heading back to England after the game so we made one last visit to Greasy Joe's. It had its usual contingent of England fans stuffing chips and burgers. This time the ticket situation was no problem. We decided to go on to the terraces and bought our tickets off a Spanish tout for 200 pesetas over face value. The Czechs would bring no fans because they wouldn't be able to get travel visas. A few England fans had seen a way to make some money by buying tickets to resell to England fans. But they got their fingers burnt, and it served them right. The pre-match drinking ritual took shape but it was nothing like the feeling that preceded the France game. We entered the stadium and took up our position behind the goal. One guy was asleep when we entered the ground and he slept on the terraces throughout the entire match. After the game his friends carried him from the ground – I presume to carry on sleeping.

The game went well and England won two–nil. After the match there was an explosion of emotion from the England fans. A conga was started and everybody on the terraces joined in. The Spanish riot police didn't know what to make of it. The conga snaked up the top of the terrace towards the exit. The police ran up and out of the exits to confront the England fans as they emerged on to the streets. But the conga did not emerge but turned round and came back again on to the terraces. The police also came back, unsure of what was happening. This happened three or four times until the conga eventually went out and down the road.

Everybody in the streets outside and in the bars that night was convinced that England would now win the World Cup. Keith and Kyle headed for home. I celebrated well into the small hours and the next morning headed back to San Sebastian with two Chelsea fans named Steve and Charlie whom I had met in a bar the previous evening. They hailed from Norbury in south London. Steve was only twenty-two but was already going bald; Charlie called him 'Bald Eagle' and kept slapping him on the head. They argued constantly, bickering like two old women, but they seemed genuine enough so I tagged along with them. We checked into a hotel and found out that Hickey and a few of his friends were also staying there. A few Scousers had just moved out. They had come with the intention of doing a bit of thieving, but after receiving a strong warning against it from Hickey, they had simply moved out.

The whole day was taken up with a huge game of beach football, and I really enjoyed myself. That night, however, it all went crazy. Most football fans have some club rivalry between themselves, but it all seemed to have been buried for the World Cup. The one group of fans who didn't seem to be able to bury the hatchet were Portsmouth. The same group of nutters Keith had met in Paris were in town. Portsmouth fans generally hate Southampton and refer to them as 'Scummers'. You could bet your bottom dollar that as soon as a Portsmouth fan heard a Southampton accent then a fight would start. No argument, just hit first and ask questions later. That night three Southampton fans were in a bar and in came the Portsmouth fans. The bar simply erupted. One of the Southampton fans was thrown bodily out of the window. Miraculously he was not seriously hurt and got up and started to run. Two of the Portsmouth fans followed him out into the road and started to kick the living daylights out of him. The two Southampton supporters left in the bar were getting belted all around the place. The whole bar was getting smashed to pieces and chairs were thrown around smashing all the glass and bottles behind the bar. The riot police turned up and started clubbing hell out of every Englishman in sight, including the poor Southampton fans. The police arrested every Englishman they could lay their hands on, even innocent fans walking along the road.

Word travelled fast, and it soon got back to the Twickenham bar that the riot police were raiding bars and arresting and beating up England fans. I was sitting quietly with the owner and his sister in the Twickenham, staying hidden in case Smiler walked in. Next moment the double doors burst open and two riot police charged in. They had hand-held machine guns and they trained them on the bar. Everyone stood stock still and went deadly quiet. More riot police rushed down the stairs, clubbing everybody in sight. The Spanish police had hate in their blows, and seemed to enjoy it. The governor moved round so they couldn't see me, and I kept down. Then the police left, taking a couple of guys away with them, and after their departure everyone was in a state of shock. There didn't seem to have been any reason for the actions of the police. People were comparing bruises, and some even started laughing, saying that it would give them some stories to tell the folks back home.

I decided to go back to my hotel but was wary about walking the streets. On leaving the bar I made my way carefully, ducking in and out of dark doorways, every sound of a car engine putting the fear of God into me, my eyes peeled for police vans. The walk back to my hotel was long and slow, but it was better than getting a beating. I spotted an England fan staggering down the road. He had had a good night out and was obviously ignorant of what was going on. 'Over here, mate,' I called out. He came over.

'What's up?' he slurred.

'Listen, mate, the riot police are beating the hell out of all England fans so get off the streets.'

'Cheers, pal,' he said, and staggered off into the night air oblivious of my concern.

I got back to my hotel and had a good night's rest. The following morning I went out on to the streets where an uneasy calm had settled on the place. Riot police were patrolling in force, looking at us. On the seafront promenade I saw two of the guys who had been taken away from the Twickenham bar by the police the previous night.

'What happened to you? You okay?'

'Yeah, they took us down the police station and threw us down the stairs and generally beat us up, then left us for a couple of hours and then chucked us out. As far as we know the only people being held are the Portsmouth fans.'

They showed me their bruises, and one had a juicy cut eye which had been stitched.

'Who stitched your eye?' I asked.

'A doctor at the police station.'

A crowd gathered and we all began talking, but the riot police told us we must disperse so we went our separate ways. I decided to go for something to eat, and headed for a restaurant. Spotting a nice exterior, I decided to go in. The restaurant was down a series of steps and as I entered I saw a lot more English fans in there.

'All right, lads, what's the food like?' I asked.

'Not bad. Don't get many chips, though,' someone replied. I burst out laughing. Here we were in the heart of Spain and all these guys could think about was chips. They came from

Bolton, and a couple of them were wearing 'Northerners Rule' T-shirts. I couldn't resist a bit of fun.

'Do they do meat and potato pie?' I asked.

'You must be joking, mate, it's paella or nothing here.'

'With chips, of course?'

'Of course!'

'Where you from, pal?'

'Surrey.'

'Who's your team?'

'Arsenal.'

One of the Bolton fans looked at me really seriously. 'Do you know Charlie Ironingboard?'

'Pardon?'

'Charlie Ironingboard, leader of Arsenal. I've met him.'

'Are you winding me up?' I asked.

'No, mate, there were three of them in a bar in Bilbao telling us they were Arsenal.'

I looked at them. There were about ten of them and I doubt if any of them was over eighteen years old. I thought that my friends the three Chelsea fans had been up to their tricks again. The poor guy continued, a little peeved that I had not believed him. 'He's called Charlie Ironingboard because he hits rival fans in the face with an old-fashioned flat-iron.' I excused myself and went to the toilet where I burst out laughing. I didn't want to shatter the illusions of these impressionable young football fans. I came back in and sat down.

'Well, do you know Charlie Ironingboard then?' they asked again.

'I don't go to many matches so I don't know the real faces,' I replied.

I didn't speak to them again and settled down to read the *Guardian* newspaper I had bought from the news-stand. The restaurant was covered in pictures of the local football team, Real Sociedad. To the Basques football is a way of expressing their identity, and to the owners of this restaurant it was obviously very important. Just above the heads of the ten Bolton fans was a T-shirt pinned to the wall. It had the crest of the Real Sociedad team on the front and when the Spanish people were not looking one of the guys pinched it. They all left shortly afterwards. I sat down and enjoyed a lovely meal but declined a side order of chips! I'm sure the owner thought that every Englishman must eat chips or he will be ill. As I was paying, the owner's wife came over to me and presented me with a keyring. On the front was the crest of arms of the Real Sociedad team and on the back was the name and address of the restaurant. It was a lovely gesture and I felt a little ashamed that I had not stopped the Bolton fans from stealing the T-shirt. What would she think of English people when she realised what they had done?

I left the restaurant and decided to go back across the border into France. I knew a lovely town called St Jean de Luz, and after a short train journey I arrived there late in the afternoon. I walked into a seafront bar and bumped straight into Gravel Voice Dave and his Oldham pals.

'Ginger!' he shouted out.

'Gravel Voice!'

'Where's Keith? I don't want another smack in the face.'

'It's all right, he's back in England.'

Gravel Voice bought me a drink and I came and sat with them outside the bar.

'What you been up to, Ginger?'

I told them all about the aggro in San Sebastian the previous night, and they told me St Jean was a great laugh. There had been no trouble in the town, but the price of beer was a lot higher than in Spain.

'Where you staying?'

'Nowhere. I must find a hotel.'

'Don't worry, you can jump in with us. There's a spare bed in one of our rooms.'

Great. That had solved the problem of carting my luggage around looking for a hotel room. The conversation and beer began to flow and the night settled in on the town, which was charming and picturesque. One of Gravel Voice's mates started chatting to me.

'Have you had the pox yet?'

'No, why should I?'

'Everyone who went up the red-light district that night after the French game caught a dose.'

I looked at him. 'I reckon you're winding me up. Oi, Gravel Voice, you lot got the pox?'

'Not all of us, but three of us have got symptoms and we're all going for a check-up in Bilbao. We've heard on the grapevine that hospital treatment for VD is free for England fans during the World Cup, so we're going to hospital before the Kuwait match.'

The guys who didn't have VD symptoms found it hilarious, as I did, especially because of the fact that if they got penicillin treatment they wouldn't be able to drink. 'Imagine winning the World Cup and celebrating on orange juice,' someone shouted across the room. It's amazing how alcohol makes everything seem amusing, and the VD was soon forgotten as the beer flowed. In fact, the biggest gripe that night and the rest of the stay in France was the price of beer.

Later in the evening a drunken bet was struck between two friends. One bet the other 50 francs he would run off the end of the pier and into the sea. Normally this is just a wind-up and the one who is supposed to do the dare stops at the last minute, but tonight this guy shouted 'Geronimo!' and jumped off the end of the pier and into the sea. Unfortunately this area is where the fishing boats come in, and he returned to the bar covered in oil and seaweed. It would have cost him substantially more than 50 francs for new clothes.

I stayed in France for the three days leading up to the

Kuwait match and found the daily drinking ritual and 'Get your tits out for the lads' songs every time a pretty French girl walked past a little boring. I decided to return to England immediately after the match and return to Spain if England reached the final. After the game, which finished one–nil to England, I scrounged a lift back to St Jean de Luz and decided to grab a bite to eat in the thirty minutes before my train was due. I had to catch that one as the only other trains before morning were sleeper trains on which you had to pay an extra fare.

I ordered the three-course set menu. The waiter brought the soup and I ordered my two other courses to be served together. He threw his arms up in the air to reason with me, but when he saw the speed at which I was downing the soup he gave up and rushed off in disgust. The second and third courses duly came out together and I bolted them down. When I had finished I noticed that a young French couple next to me, who had sat down at the same time, were just starting their soup. As I turned to leave I saw them looking at me and shaking their heads.

'It's all right, I'm an English football fan.'

Their expression changed from bewilderment to understanding. They nodded and smiled as if to say, 'Only an English football fan could treat food like that.' To cap it all, I even had chips that night.

I arrived at the train station one minute late, just in time to see the departing train's rear red light. French railways, unlike British Rail, run on time. The rush in eating my food and the run for the train had left me feeling very ill. The sleeper was not due for forty-five minutes and during the wait two young England fans from Birmingham came on to the platform. We all decided to try to get a sleeping compartment without paying, but no sooner had I got on the train than the guard grabbed hold of me. The other two, though, got away with it.

I headed back to England broke but happy, and convinced I would be returning in a fortnight for the final. No matter how good the trip, it is always a great feeling coming back to England, and all football fans returning from foreign trips feel the same. Meanwhile, the other England fans headed for Madrid where they found the social climate quite different. Fans sleeping in the park were attacked and robbed by Madrid street gangs. The police were openly hostile, and on the day of one match brutally attacked a bar full of England fans.

I never did get my chance to return to Spain, for England were eliminated, failing to win their games against Spain and West Germany.

7

Robson's Boys

After the World Cup, Ron Greenwood, the England manager, retired and Bobby Robson took over. Robson's first game as manager was in Copenhagen. England drew two–all but that fact was forgotten as the England fans created absolute havoc. It is not well known that the Danish street gangs wanted to get in on the action right from the start. The general behaviour of the England fans, though, was quite despicable. I wasn't there, but all those who were present will tell you the same. Here the hooligans turned up because they knew the Danish authorities would merely deport any fans found guilty of misconduct at the match. And so it proved.

The next big game for any England fan worth his salt was in Budapest. The game was played on 12 October 1983, and was generally regarded as the best punch-up ever had on the Continent. It is not yet common knowledge but football fans behind the Iron Curtain have punch-ups at football matches. The Budapest fans who caused the aggro were supporters of Ferencvaros, the local Budapest team. England fans turned up on the train and as they all got off at the Nep stadium station the Hungarians were waiting for them. The England fans, and especially the Chelsea supporters, thought this was great fun and an almighty confrontation ensued. It was fist and boot, and for those present a great time was had by all. The police turned up and broke it up, but it has still gone down as the number one punch-up.

This was also the game when Hickey and his pals stitched up the Football Association committee. The FA people, and especially Ted Croker, the Secretary, are really extremely patronising and do not like England fans travelling. They have never bothered to try to sort out the genuine fans or make them feel welcome. Hickey and the Chelsea fans were not popular, partly because of their blatant racist views (with which I do not agree) and partly because of their anti-social behaviour. Chelsea fans have the habit of drinking in the bar of the particular hotel where the England team are staying. This infuriates the FA officials who, in my opinion, take a completely pompous attitude. It is also a great way for fans to try to pick up tickets. Sometimes a naïve player will organise some complimentary tickets – usually a small-club player who doesn't really know he is supposed to be above a travelling fan.

On this particular day one of the Chelsea fans approached the FA people, who were in the foyer of the Intercontinental. They had a table set up and the system was that people who were on the list could pick up tickets. The Chelsea fan went up to the desk and enquired whether there were any spare tickets. He was asked his name and the FA man went through his list. When the name was not found on the list he said gleefully. 'No, and you won't get in because the match is sold out.'

The Chelsea fan had noticed a name on the list and he walked back to the bar and said to his friend, 'Go up to the desk and say you are V. Brown.' He did this and got V.

Brown's tickets, at the same time picking out another name on the list. This went on until all the Chelsea fans in the bar had tickets. The drink flowed all afternoon and when Ted Croker came down into the foyer looking smug he was greeted with the Chelsea fans waving the tickets in the air with shouts of, 'Look what we've got, Ted!' The FA officials were left with red faces.

After the game the fun continued. The Ferencvaros fans wanted to have a go at the England fans but were stopped by the police. The England fans, led by Hickey with a map, walked around the streets and came out behind the Ferencvaros fans and everyone had a really good punch-up again. Hickey was nicknamed 'General Hickey' by some northern fans. His reputation was made. As well as this, there was also the scene of scores of England fans storming out of the Intercontinental hotel for a punch-up, then returning casually to the bar for a drink.

The climax of the European Championship's qualifying competition was coming up. England were playing Luxembourg away. The same day Denmark were playing in Greece and if Denmark won they would qualify for the European Championships in France in the coming summer. Both games were being played at the same time on 16 November 1983. I had made plans to go to the England match with Keith Chitty. The Luxembourg authorities were very nervous about having thousands of England fans in the tiny principality, especially if Denmark won – although the media were predicting that Greece would win. A lot of England fans were going to travel. The scene was set for a confrontation.

Dave Kelly is a nutter, Leatherhead's equivalent of Smiler, but at that time I didn't know this. I learned his nickname was 'No Marbles', due to his conspicuous lack of brains. Keith had decided to travel to Luxembourg with his fiancée, Sandra, so I decided to travel alone; but Dave Kelly made up his mind to travel with me. I didn't know how crazy he was until the night before I left and Sammy White approached me in my local pub.

'Are you going to Luxembourg with Kelly?'

'Yes, why do you ask?'

'Because he'll get you both locked up.'

I had arranged to meet Kelly at Leatherhead station and we were travelling down to Dover for the overnight ferry to Ostend. The train journey to Dover was uneventful. I met a few people on the train and from what I could see every thug in England had decided to travel to Luxembourg. Kelly and I bought some beer and he started drinking as soon as the train left Victoria. The police, mindful that trouble might erupt, were waiting at Dover, and some also got on to the ferry. The ship departed and as usual everyone made their way to the bar at the front. But the captain had decided, under police advice, not to open the bar. I could see this was counter-productive, because the duty-free shops would still be open and the idiots would be drinking spirits instead of beer. I even went down and spoke to the captain, but he had made up his mind. Sure enough, the idiots went into the duty-free shop and bought plenty of spirits. Kelly bought a litre bottle of Bacardi and half a bottle of gin. This was on top of the six cans of McEwan's Export he had bought in Leatherhead.

The boat berthed at Ostend, to be met by a huge contingent of Belgian riot police. The British police felt smug and clever because they had kept the bars shut and, they felt, avoided trouble, but most people had slept on the ferry anyway. There was plenty of time for drinking over the next forty-eight hours, so why get pissed on the ferry and be refused entry to Belgium?

Everyone boarded trains under the watchful eye of the police. Next stop Brussels. The train arrived at about 7 a.m. and by this time Kelly had teamed up with a particularly odious character called Peter, who had no money and no gear and was intending to live on his wits for two days. At Brussels there was a bar on the concourse, and a lot of people went over and had a drink while waiting for the train to Luxembourg. Kelly went over with Peter and ordered a beer.

'Oi, you Belgian whore, give us a lager!' shouted Kelly.

'Yeah, slag, pour the beer,' joined Peter.

The Belgian woman spoke back in Flemish, but she knew what they were saying. They continued in the same vein, thinking it was really funny, and other England fans soon joined in this great sport. It is not unusual for England fans to act like this abroad, but I find it distasteful in the extreme.

I went for a walk round the station to see who was about. I noticed a big group of Scousers milling around, and I spoke to one of them. They had been thieving in Brussels and they knew that it would be even easier pickings in Luxembourg. I walked back across to the bar and heard Kelly being very loud. Just at that moment Keith and Sandra walked up to me. They had purposely avoided Kelly and didn't realise he had come with me. Kelly also spotted Keith and Sandra and came over. 'Hello, Sandra, give us a kiss!' he shouted. Sandra flushed bright red with embarrassment and told Keith she wanted to sit down somewhere. They made their excuses and left. By now Kelly was getting extremely loud. I was pleased when the train arrived and we boarded. I made my way through the carriages and found two seats. Kelly sat down.

'Oi, Kelly, don't drink all that drink or else you'll be out of the game by Luxembourg.'

Kelly took no notice, but opened up the half-bottle of gin and started mixing it with orange juice. 'This will dilute it,' he said.

The Belgian people already on board the train looked at us anxiously. This was the cream of English hooliganism.

Kelly finished the gin and immediately opened the Bacardi, swigging back the bottle. 'I'm going for a walk down the train,' he said.

'All right, mate, see you later.'

He walked off and I started playing cards with four Southampton fans. A young England fan climbed on to the luggage rack, stretched out and went to sleep. The Belgian passengers looked at him in absolute horror. The guard walked through but did not notice him. Half an hour later Kelly staggered back. He had demolished a third of the Bacardi and was very drunk.

'Go easy, Dave.'

'Stop worrying, Ginger, you sound like my mum.'

Two pretty girls were sitting across from us and Kelly spotted them. He leaned over them; God only knows what his breath smelt like.

'Hello, girls, fancy a drink?' They looked frightened.

'Come on, girls, have a drop of this,' he said, offering them the Bacardi bottle.

'Leave it out, Dave,' I said.

'What's the matter, girls, don't you fancy me? You think I'm pissed, don't you?'

'Dave, they don't think, they know you're pissed. Now leave them alone and go back up the train,' I said.

Kelly staggered off again with all the other passengers whispering as he walked past. Occasionally he would stop and offer some poor Belgian a drink. One of the Southampton fans turned to me.

'Your mate is going to be in a right state by the time we get to Luxembourg.'

I agreed and decided to walk up the train and have a few strong words with him. I entered a carriage through the automatic doors and Kelly was standing on a seat in full flow. He was providing the entertainment for the whole carriage of England fans. I went up to him and grabbed him. 'Kelly, now listen here. I'm warning you, if you drink that whole bottle then I'll have nothing to do with you.' People in the carriage were jeering at me; after all, I had ended the cabaret. One guy with a Manchester accent shouted at me, 'Don't be a spoilsport, pal, let him get on with it.' I stormed over to him. 'You can piss off. If you enjoy his company so much then you look after him when we get to Luxembourg.'

I turned and walked out of the carriage, with Kelly shouting, 'Come on, Ginger, I'm only having a little drink. Fellow Arsenal fans shouldn't fall out.' I could hear the roars as Kelly took another swig at the bottle while I walked away.

Once back in my seat I continued to play cards. I forgot about Kelly and just concentrated on my poker hands. Just before we got to Luxembourg I saw an incident which summed up the English fan mentality. We were sitting in a non-smoking carriage. Notices were everywhere, but still English guys lit up. One was puffing away as the guard came through, and a Belgian woman sitting with her husband pointed it out. The guard walked over and asked for his ticket, pointing out to him in Flemish that it was a non-smoking carriage.

'I don't speak that foreign crap. Speak in English, you moron!' shouted the England fan. The guard looked at his ticket, snatched it from the fan, and walked away down the train.

'Oi, you wanker, that's a return, bring it back!'

Two Leeds fans sitting further down the train grabbed the guard and took the ticket off him, returning it to its owner. The guard retreated, but the England fan did put out his cigarette. (When the train finally arrived in Luxembourg, the woman who had complained was spat at by the England fan.)

'Right, lads, final hand,' said the Southampton guy.

'Well, deal a good one,' I replied.

The train was almost in Luxembourg when someone tapped me on the shoulder. I turned round and standing in front of me was someone I didn't know. 'Your pal Kelly has collapsed and is unconscious.'

'What happened?'

'Everyone bet him he couldn't drink the last third of the Bacardi bottle straight down – but he did, and he collapsed. You'd better come and get him.'

I grabbed him by the lapels on his coat. 'Listen here, you had the fun out of him so you get him to an ambulance. Now clear off.'

He turned and walked away, and I looked for Keith and Sandra.

'Keith, Kelly's collapsed.'

'Bollocks to Kelly! He's a nutter!' he shouted to me, and hurried off the train and up the platform with Sandra.

Kelly was carried off the train and thrown on a luggage trailer, then pushed along the platform. I stayed at a discreet distance, just to make sure I was not pointed out as his pal and asked to pick up the hospital bill. The guys pushed him up to a large contingent of riot police who had met the train. One look at him and they quickly summoned medical assistance. Kelly was rushed to hospital to have his stomach pumped. The look on the faces of the riot police told the whole story: their nightmares were coming true, the savages had arrived. Luxembourg was under siege. What would the next forty-eight hours hold for them?

I proceeded out of the station and up the road. I stepped into a bar and met a couple of interesting guys. One was called Paul, the other Bud. Paul was just twenty-one, worked in Berlin and was, like myself, an Arsenal supporter.

Bud was six feet tall, swarthy, and had a Zapata moustache. He had been to Luxembourg the last time England had played there, and said that the place to go was Barbarellas, but it was shut and during the time we were there it stayed shut. The three of us sat at the bar ordering beer and chatting. Paul had nowhere to stay and suggested we share a room. We walked about the streets but most hotels and guest houses had 'full' notices in the windows. I couldn't believe they were all full, and indeed, one guest house proprietor who spoke perfect English confirmed my suspicions. He told me that the Luxembourg people had seen on TV the destruction England fans had caused everywhere, and a prominent newspaper had condemned the Luxembourg authorities for allowing the match to go ahead in the city. I said to him, 'Not all Englishmen are the same.'

'Come back and tell me in forty-eight hours; we shall see.'

We tried another hotel. I could see all the room keys hanging on the board so I knew they had vacancies. I rang the bell and a woman appeared. 'Vacancies?' I asked.

'How many?' she replied.

'Just a room for two.'

'Do you want to see it?'

'Yes, please.'

Suddenly the expression on her face changed to one of complete terror. I heard English voices coming from outside.

'In here lads, looks like a result.'

I turned and saw about twenty guys coming in the door. 'No vacancies, full up!' she screamed fearfully. I walked out quickly and turned to Paul. 'We've got to lose that lot or else we won't get anywhere.'

We were lucky in that Paul spoke German, and we got a room on the strength of that. A lot of England fans had got into hotels somehow, but now there seemed to be a block on any more. We had a quick wash and went out on the town, returning to the bar where Paul and I had been drinking earlier. Peter, the chap who had been abusing the Belgian woman with Kelly, was in the bar. Paul knew him and they began to drink together. I found Peter obnoxious because of his love of abusing foreigners, so I left and decided to visit Radio Luxembourg. I didn't have a match ticket but I went into a newsagents and they were selling them across the counter. I bought one, but as I went to leave the shop I saw two England fans come in the door, grab a load of confectionery and run out again. It was all over in a flash, but I felt extremely embarrassed. The shock of seeing such blatant thieving made me wonder what the local people would think of us.

As I walked past a restaurant I heard a bang on the window. I looked up to see Keith and Sandra, so I walked in and up to their table and sat down.

'Where's Kelly?' asked Keith.

'In hospital, having his stomach pumped.'

'How much did he drink?' asked Sandra.

'Six cans of McEwans, half a bottle of gin and a litre of Bacardi.'

Keith burst out laughing.

'I think his luggage has gone to Switzerland,' I said.

'What about his passport?' asked Sandra.

'That's in Switzerland too.'

We decided not to talk about Kelly and left the restaurant to go and see if we could have a look round Radio Luxembourg. But when we got there, the girl on reception would have none of it.

'I am a famous disc jockey in England,' I said.

She passed a sticker through the hatch. At that moment a real English disc jockey who worked on the station came in the door. 'All right, mate?' I said.

'Hello. Here for the match?' he asked.

'Yeah. Any chance of a tour of the station?'

'Any other time perhaps, but not until all the England fans have left. The Luxembourg authorities are frightened of trouble.'

We walked out into the cold night air. It was mid-

November and there was a definite chill. The city looked grey and bleak, and the colours of the buildings seemed to sum up its mood. It was a city living in fear. We walked down to the ground and popped into a bar. A few England fans were sitting on bar stools. A few of them had had a lot to drink and were explaining that they had nowhere to stay. Keith had discovered a middle-aged Portuguese guy and was doing his party piece with him. He was reciting the England 1966 World Cup team and laughing at the older man's pronunciation. I have seen Keith do this on many occasions and it can be quite funny.

'Gordon Banks!' shouted Keith.

'Bobby Charlton!' shouted back the Portuguese.

Keith pulled a face to insinuate ugliness, and shouted, 'Nobby Stiles!'

At this point the foreigners usually burst out laughing and gesticulate to indicate that Nobby had no teeth. Of course we know this, and it makes for a bit of fun. Keith always does it in good part and once he gets a bar full of foreigners going it really is pure theatre. After the name recital he will then go through a goal that Bobby Charlton has scored. On this particular night the other England fans in the bar thought this was the funniest sight they had ever seen – one of them even fell off his stool but was still laughing when he hit the ground.

The Portuguese chap went out to his car to fetch a football. He wanted to show us the goal that was scored in the 1966 World Cup Final in extra time – the famous one from Geoff Hurst that possibly didn't cross the line. Chalk was used, and everyone joined in the argument, including some people walking past. Keith shouted out 'Paul van Hinst!' (a famous Belgian footballer), and everyone wanted to shake his hand. The Portuguese guy left the bar gesticulating wildly, but returned ten minutes later with his wife. He asked us to go with them, so Keith and I, along with Sandra who was frightened we would get our throats cut, left the bar, which was still in uproar.

The Portuguese guy took us to see his son, who spoke good English and lived in a very attractive house. He explained to us that his father would consider it a great honour if we would dine in his house. I accepted gladly, but Keith had to talk Sandra into it. We went to his house and his wife cooked us a meal while we all consumed large quantities of wine. The poor woman was not amused as her husband, Keith and I went through every footballer who had ever put on a pair of boots. Sandra was getting filthy looks from the wife and began to feel uncomfortable, so we decided to leave. It took us about fifteen minutes to say goodbye, and Keith promised to take him to the match the following night. I had been around his house, met his family, eaten at his home and still I didn't know his name. As we left his house and made our way across the freezing ground back to the centre of town I suddenly realised that his wife had not bothered to say goodbye to us. I bet the man took some verbal abuse that night.

Keith and Sandra headed for their hotel. It was gone midnight, but I didn't feel like sleeping yet. Although it was late and the temperature had dropped below freezing, English fans were standing around talking. I struck up a conversation with some fellow Londoners.

'Anywhere to get a drink?' I asked.

'Most places are shut,' they replied.

A shifty-looking guy approached us. 'Looking for a drink? Woman perhaps?' he asked in accented English.

'Yeah, where?' I replied.

'Follow me,' he said

'You coming, lads?' I asked the Londoners.

'No, Ginger, you go ahead. I bet it's rubbish.'

I followed the small guy up a narrow street, surveying him from head to toe. He was about five foot eight, slim and reasonably well dressed. I looked behind me in case it was a set-up, but I didn't think it was. He walked up to a door and banged on it twice. The door opened and I was ushered in. Once inside I noticed a small bar with two women serving beer to about thirty or so England fans. There were small lamps on the wall giving out a dim light, and sitting in the darkness were three women and a guy. As I looked at them the man beckoned me to go over. I ordered a beer and went across to him. He spoke English, but not well, and looked a typical Belgian with the customary moustache.

'These are my girls. Want to join them?'

'Depends how much.'

'Three thousand Belgian francs.'

'Fifty quid? You must be joking.'

He smiled at me. 'English not so rich; you stick to drinking, eh?'

I returned to the bar and struck up a conversation with two overweight Yorkshiremen. They were Huddersfield supporters, and had nowhere to stay. They told me that they hoped this bar would stay open all night so that they could prop it up. I didn't blame them, for it was freezing outside. They spoke to me loudly and I took the mickey out of their accents.

'You bloody Cockneys are all piss-takers. I suppose you're Chelsea. I bloody hate Chelsea.'

A couple of young guys were drinking next to us and heard the remark. They walked over.

'What did you say, you northern div?' one asked.

'Leave it out, they were having a joke,' I said.

'I do bloody hate Chelsea,' said the Yorkshireman – but in fun, not aggressively.

The two Chelsea fans, for that's what they were, squared up. They were barely nineteen years old and didn't look very tough, but one of them was holding his hand inside his coat as if he had a knife. I looked at him. 'You aren't going to pull a blade in here, and we both know it,' I said. The other fan punched the Yorkshireman but it barely brushed his head. I grabbed him and pushed him back. 'I said leave it out.'

The two Yorkshiremen didn't want to fight – they were just friendly big-mouths – but if a fight had started they would have slaughtered the two young Chelsea fans. I don't think they had an ounce of malice in them, but the woman behind the bar had seen the punch thrown and decided to shut the bar. The two Chelsea fans left in a huff, glaring at the three of us. I turned to the two Yorkshiremen. 'Sit tight, they might serve us a beer in a minute.'

The guy sitting in the corner with the three girls stood up and came over. 'No more drink. Englishmen want to fight.'

'Come on, mate. The two hotheads have left.'

We pleaded with him to serve us some more beer, but he wouldn't listen. The three of us were the last to leave the bar. I scurried back to my hotel feeling a bit peeved, leaving the Yorkshiremen to sort out the best way of finding accommodation. The next day I bumped into them and they told me that they had found a strip club, gone in, bought one beer and fell asleep. The owner had let them sleep until seven the next morning. When I got back to my hotel there was chaos. Some England fans had thrown a wardrobe down the stairs and police were in the hotel arresting and arguing with everyone. I finally got to bed at three in the morning.

I was rudely awoken at seven the next morning by Peter, who was washing his face in the sink next to my bed.

'Oi, what are you doing in here?'

'Paul let me jump in the room.'

'Piss off, you ponce, you have just woken me up.'

I was annoyed, mostly because I didn't like him. He didn't offer me any money for staying in the room – but that just summed him up.

I got dressed and left Paul and Peter to their own devices. On the streets the police and army were putting on a show of strength. I walked down to the railway station where England fans were still arriving. I stood on the pavement talking to different people, trying to find out what had been happening. Rumour was that a jeweller's shop had been done, and also that if England didn't qualify then all hell was going to break loose. I knew that a large contingent of West Ham fans was in town, but I was most surprised when I saw other London fans with them, even a few Millwall. Most of them were drinking further up the town in Club 42. I decided to give it a wide berth and settled down in a little bar with some other Arsenal fans, where I heard that there had been trouble on a train between Cockneys and Manchester United supporters.

This is the part of away travel that I enjoy the most – sitting in a bar and just spending time in small talk. There is no rush to down the beer and you hear some wonderful stories and meet some real characters. As you may have noticed, I have a tendency to nickname people, and when a guy who looked like Tony Woodcock (the Arsenal footballer) walked into the bar, it wasn't very long before everyone was chanting 'Woody, Woody'. The bar we were in was very popular, and about mid-afternoon Hickey turned up and stood outside where a big crowd was gathering. The army and police thought it was time to shut the bar, and came in. 'No more beer in this bar,' the army captain said, and told the proprietors to shut down. Everyone went outside and was milling around. The army, looking smart and carrying big truncheons, were very nervous. The captain of this particular group had a pair of specs; he came over to the group. 'You must all disperse. We cannot allow big groups to hang around the streets.'

'You shouldn't have shut the bars then, you stupid pillock,' someone shouted.

A few army men walked past; all had at least one stripe, some two. A sharp-eyed Londoner spotted this. 'Oi, captain, don't you have any privates in your army?' he shouted out. Everyone burst out laughing. A few people started saluting the army and shouting 'Attention!' and '*Sieg Heil*!' It was a tense situation, but all of a sudden everyone just walked off in different directions. The army stood perplexed, not knowing which group to follow. I went for a walk on my own and bumped into a few faces I knew and people I'd met the previous night. Fat Graham approached me. He was an overweight Chelsea fan who went to all England games.

'All right, Ginger?'

'Yes, fine. Where's everyone drinking?'

'Near Club 42.'

'What's up there?'

'A few of the guys are going to do the Giorgio Armani shop later on. They've already cased it out. Are you coming up there with us?'

'No, it's not my scene.'

I left, found a quiet bar and had a drink with a couple of other people who, like myself, didn't like the mood that was spreading among the England fans. If we didn't qualify then this city would be wrecked; win or lose, certain groups were going to use the occasion to loot and steal. I left the bar at about 5.30 and decided to go for a stroll around the city. The faces of the Luxembourg residents told the story. They were nervous and fearful of the coming night. The army didn't seem to know what to do. Most England fans had been drinking and were in a good mood. Everybody knew we would beat Luxembourg, and we just hoped Greece would help us out against Denmark.

As I approached the traffic lights near the ground I spotted a huge group of fans. They were the 'wild bunch', and were walking across cars, helping themselves to food in shops and generally terrorising the inhabitants. A security van pulled up at the lights and stopped alongside them. In a flash a young England fan opened the back door. The van was stuck, as there was a car in front of him. The driver suddenly realised what was happening. He quickly manoeuvred to his left and accelerated through the red light. Cars coming in other directions were forced to brake and swerve. He shot off up the road with his door banging away, wide open. I don't think anything was taken but this seemed to inflame the mood of the fans, who smashed the window of a petrol station when the owner would not let them into the shop. I moved away from them and cut across some waste ground. Again I bumped into Keith and Sandra.

'Hello, Keith.'

'Hello, Ginger. Kelly's dead.'

'Don't be silly. Who told you that?'

'One of the blokes who was with him on the train.'

'I don't believe it.'

I felt awful. What would his family say to me? I felt responsible and hoped against hope it wasn't true. We walked down the road to the ground, and there, standing outside the entrance, was Kelly, looking dreadfully pale. For the first time on the trip I was really pleased to see him.

We entered the ground together. The ground itself is very small, and the England fans were all gathered at one end surrounded by barbed wire, metal fences and riot police. Parts of the terraces were shut off and were full of police. The back of the terraces has a walkway, and we walked to the far end and stood next to the fence in front of the corner flag. Some people had radios and were listening for news of the match in Greece. Denmark had scored two goals. It didn't matter what happened here; England were out.

The mood on the terraces became violent. Despite England scoring two early goals, people started trying to pull down fences at the front. I went to the back of the terraces and saw a large group of England fans leave the stadium. It was at the back of the terraces that all the action was happening. All feuds and battles were back on; inter-club rivalries would not now be forgotten. I stood at the back of the terrace on my own and laughed at the irony of it all. We had come all this way to have a party, yet it had been spoilt by events hundreds of miles away. I heard a voice nearby and looked up. In front of me were four people, one of whom was snarling at me. He had a moustache and a northern accent, was in his early twenties and was stockily built.

'What are you laughing at?'

'I'm laughing because I think it's funny.'

'What's funny?'

'All of us standing here, being upstaged by a little country called Denmark.'

I could see that he was going to hit me, and he had three other people with him. I decided to give it my best shot. I didn't realise it, but the big group of London fans had got together and were attacking and beating groups of northern fans. A couple of them had spotted the four picking on me. I didn't see them approach and the scowling face in front of me changed to one of shock and pain as a punch hit him on the side of the head. His eyes rolled around in their sockets and he staggered forward and dropped on to one knee just in front of me. His friends all ran as the Londoners went into them. The Cockneys, tired of the chase after ten yards, turned and walked back past me. They were laughing.

'Cheers, lads,' I said.

'No problem, mate, any time,' one replied, and continued walking.

One of the group, which consisted of Chelsea, West Ham and Millwall fans, walked over and kicked the kneeling fan in the ribs.

'Go on, mate, give him a dig. After all, he was gonna do you.'

I looked at the poor fellow, who was on all fours but was trying to get up. I walked over and pulled him up by his lapels.

'I'm still laughing, mate. How about you?'

With that I punched him in the stomach and let him go, leaving him to slump to his knees once more. I decided to go and stand near the London fans as it seemed safer, and I had a conversation with a couple of them. Then I went to the toilet, which was underneath the terraces. I walked down the concrete steps just behind a fan who, I noticed, had MUFC (which stands for Manchester United Football Club) tattooed on his hand. He went up to the urinal and as he stood there a Londoner, who must have followed us in, came up behind him and kicked his legs away. He hit the urine-covered floor with a sickening thud. Three guys then set about him with their boots, one hitting him in the side of the head and causing it to jerk violently back and strike the wall behind the urinal. I thought the kick had killed him, but he still had his wits and curled up against the wall plumbing. The three Londoners were in no rush, and stood back picking their spots to aim at. I just ignored the assault, as did two others who were in the toilet at the same time. But one other guy tried to leave. He was barely twenty years old and petrified. One Londoner confronted him.

'Where are you from?'

'Birmingham,' he replied, the fear evident in his voice.

'Birmingham supporter are we? I fuckin' hate Birmingham. '

'No, mate.'

'Don't tell me: you don't go to watch any team regularly.'

The Londoner knew the poor guy was frightened out of his mind, and was enjoying the sight of him shaking. The two other Cockneys had tired of kicking the prostrate and motionless Mancunian and walked over. One of them grabbed the young fan by the hair.

'Do you fuckin' want some?'

I turned and walked up to them. 'Come on, just get the main faces. You know the people you're after.'

The one who had hold of his hair looked at me. His face broke into a smile. 'You struck lucky, pal?' he said, looking at the young and frightened fan. We walked up the steps and the guy from Birmingham thanked me. I don't know what happened to the Mancunian who had taken a bad kicking. I was just pleased to get out of that toilet.

All through the rest of the game it was the same: any non-London fans were going to get it. For the first time at a football match I felt really fearful of what might happen. The vicious kicking handed out to the Mancunian had shocked me. The final whistle went and everybody surged out of the ground. The riot police tried to keep everyone together, but splinter groups just broke away. I had never seen anything like it. Most people were determined to smash and destroy. The group I was following threw a road-works sign at a police motorcyclist, causing him to fall off. Within seconds he was being kicked, and one young fan tried to steal his gun. The riot police charged in to save him. Windows were being smashed with bricks, and the looters saw their chance.

A road sign went straight through the middle of the window and the rest of it was knocked out by a couple of others with big lumps of wood. Two people moved in with cardboard boxes and filled them with jumpers, best cashmere Giorgio Armani. These would be highly resaleable back in England. Chancers who were going past dived in and grabbed jumpers. It was all over in less than two minutes. People were waiting round the corner and the booty was put into holdall bags. Everyone dispersed and agreed to meet up later at the train station. The two bag-carriers went on their way – two mugs who had to do as they were told. They just liked the thrill of hanging round hard men and nutters.

It was then that the plan went wrong. The two bag-carriers walked into a street and a riot van came down it in the opposite direction. The carriers lost their nerve, dropped the bags and ran, leaving the riot police to retrieve the jumpers. I saw the same two on the corner of the main street by Club 42. They were frightened to go back to the meeting place because they had lost the gear. I left them looking very scared.

The Scousers, many of whom had left the ground during the match, were concentrating on the jewellers' shops and a good few were looted. People who were probably law-abiding citizens at any other time just went berserk. The faces of people as they went into a smashed shop and grabbed goods were amazing: all signs of reason had disappeared from their eyes. One guy came out of a shop with his eyes rolled up, his tongue hanging from an open mouth and breathing heavily. His trip into the shop had been positively a physical experience, and he was beginning to smile. He had dared and won. Others, of course, were not so lucky and were grabbed by riot police. Later they would all plead their innocence to the watching world. In a very short space of time the streets of Luxembourg had been transformed into a madhouse. Sirens blared out and police vans screeched around the cobbled streets.

Back on the open space in front of the station the police were searching bags to try to find out who had stolen goods. I think it was only a token display; they had shut the stable door after the horse had bolted. I decided to cross the border out of Luxembourg and wait elsewhere for a train. I ended up in a bar in Aarlon, in Belgium. About ten or so England fans were in there and we were approached by two Belgians who asked us if we wanted a laugh. Three of us went with them and ended up back in Luxembourg, being chased by the police through the city centre at three in the morning. One of the Belgians was a rally driver, and he made the police look silly. Unfortunately, he also frightened the pants off us. I was more frightened in his car than I had been earlier in the toilets at the ground.

The next morning I arrived in Brussels and decided to go for something to eat. I sat down in a restaurant and got chatting to some Scousers.

'What did you get last night?' they asked.

'Nothing. It's not my scene.'

'Want to buy any gear? Watches, chains, good gold – eighteen-carat stuff?'

I laughed and declined the offer. I thought they might have some trouble at British Customs, but they told me they would stash the gear at Ostend in the left luggage lockers and return in a week's time when the heat had died down. They were all in their early twenties and I doubt if they had ever had a chance of a proper job. To them stealing was a legitimate pastime and anywhere was fair game. I didn't agree with what they had done, but I could understand their point of view.

On the way back to England Keith and Sandra bumped into Kelly at Ostend; he had not lost his passport after all. His luggage arrived back in England five weeks later. Typically, on the jetfoil travelling home Kelly got stuck into the drink once again, and totally abused all the staff on board.

The aftermath of the trouble in Luxembourg was not as bad as first feared – at least England were not banned from Europe. But I do not think any English teams will ever be allowed to play in that country again. I had seen behaviour which I never thought I would see from English football fans. On returning to England I wrote to Ted Croker, the Secretary of the Football Association, telling him that he must find a way to stop people travelling who would cause trouble on that scale. But he made the usual sort of non-committal noises. In all fairness, though, his hands are tied by the politicians. I vowed never again to follow England to an away match. However, my self-enforced ban was not to last very long, as once more the urge to travel was to take a grip.

France against England was always going to be a flash-point. Paris is too easy to get to and too full of nightlife for any hooligan to want to miss a match there. England played in Paris at the end of February 1984 and once more serious disturbances broke out. The fighting began on the ferries, between West Ham and Chelsea fans. The West Ham, encouraged by the fact that they had the numbers, started taking liberties; serious disorder broke out, and knives were brandished.

Once in Paris the St Germain skinheads were waiting for the England fans and ambushed the Métro trains with CS gas. (When someone sprays that at you, you automatically reel backwards. When it is sprayed in a tube train you are done for. Football fans learn quickly, and CS gas is often used nowadays in a raid on rival fans' public houses.) The disorder continued in the ground and despite the firm hand of the French riot police, there were disturbances in the streets afterwards and cars were overturned. This was apart from the normal, almost ritual bad behaviour displayed by English fans in France.

The Football Association officials and players normally do not hear what goes on with the fans as they stay away from them, but on one occasion it was forced home to them what morons some fans can be. It was the 1984 South American tour and England had won two–nil in Rio de Janeiro. John Barnes, who is black, had scored one of the all-time great international goals. On the plane flying to Uruguay were the officials, players and press. Also on board was a group of Chelsea fans, every one a racist. To them black players' goals don't count, so England had won one–nil. It was an absurd attitude, but everyone could hear them being boorish and pathetic. Why some of the players didn't go down and say something I don't know, but it took the press to have words with them. It didn't make any difference, but after that incident the players ignored *all* the fans, which was hard on people who had paid a lot of money to follow England and had nothing to do with the racist cant.

Later in the year England were to play in Istanbul and I was determined to see them play at the meeting of Europe and Asia. I applied for one ticket for the match and received a letter from Ted Croker saying that I had to produce this letter at the Sheraton hotel in order to pick up my ticket. They had learnt a lesson from the Hungarian experience. I bought a cheap ticket from a bucket shop in Soho and decided to travel on the Monday and return Saturday night. I found out that Hickey had organised a four-day trip, so I phoned him and discovered that his group was on the same flight as me.

It was a chilly Monday morning at Heathrow. Once checked in I went through passport control. It was only eight in the morning but already people in Hickey's group were drinking beer. I sat down and had a good chat with Hickey. Everyone was waiting for Salford and Binman. These two are a dynamic, albeit loony, duo and they go to all England games. Every penny they earn is saved for their travelling expenses. They both hail from Manchester, and Binman works on the dust-carts – hence his nickname. Salford is a staunch Protestant and often turns up on away matches dressed in jeans, T-shirt, donkey jacket and carrying a William of Orange Battle of the Boyne flag. He brings nothing else, and he stinks by the end of the trip. It was the first time I had ever seen Salford but I had heard of him. Sure enough, he arrived with his flag, but no kit. I wouldn't like to have sat next to him on the return journey. Binman, again, is not renowned for his cleanliness, which is one reason why he and Salford make a good duo.

We were all due to travel on KLM, the Dutch national airline. The flight to Istanbul was pretty normal apart from the amount of beer being drunk. It was free, and when the beer stocks were exhausted the stewardesses dished out small screw-top bottles of wine. Everyone stocked up. Salford was singing his anti-papist songs and a good few people on the plane gave us funny looks. The Dutch are a gentle people and seem to find it difficult to understand English football fans. As we disembarked at Istanbul I jumped on the coach which was taking us to the hotel. I was not officially on Hickey's tour but he told me that if any room had a spare bed I could jump in free of charge. There was a varied assortment of different football fans on the coach including Bolton, Brighton and Arsenal supporters. This was also the first time I met Terence Last, or 'Ginger Terry' as everyone called him. Terry asked me if I wanted to go to the under-21 game the next day in Bursa, which sounded like a good idea.

At the hotel I shared a room with two other Chelsea fans called Don and Steve. Steve was the stereotype of a football fan as portrayed in the press: 5 feet 10 inches tall, well built and with a beer belly. He wore T-shirts which because of his belly didn't fit him properly. His trousers had to be worn under his stomach, and consequently the top of the cheeks of his bum were frequently on parade. I always find it very funny to watch these types trying to chase after other fans, bellies wobbling outrageously. Steve was also the type of fan who, no matter what the weather, will go to a football match wearing just a T-shirt, usually with something irrelevant written on it. It could be a freezing cold day in January when most people are wrapped up warm, but you will still see one of these halfwits in his T-shirt. It makes me shiver just to look at them.

That night everyone assembled in the bar while I went out to find the Pudding Shop, made famous by the film *Midnight Express*. Istanbul is a haven for travellers of the backpacking variety, and I spent an enjoyable evening talking to some of them. A couple of them didn't even know England were due to play there the coming Wednesday. Later in the evening, as I was sitting downstairs in the Pudding Shop with a couple of backpackers, I noticed three people standing near a couple of girls. West Ham fans, I thought. The people I was with couldn't understand how I knew, but I could tell by their general demeanour. I decided to leave and drank up.

Istanbul at night is a strange place, for there are no women around. During the day you see plenty of very attractive women, but at night they disappear. The bars are full of men, and it brought back memories of the crazy Turk at Liverpool and also things I had read about the way the Turks fought in the First World War. I decided I wouldn't be getting into any fights in Istanbul. There was also the unnerving sight of the army on the streets with machine guns. The all-pervading presence of the army reminded me that military rule was in force.

One dynamic duo that came to the fore in Istanbul consisted of 'Doddy' and 'Crazy Bob'.

Doddy was mental – not a nutter like Smiler, but crazy. It was always inevitable that Doddy would team up with someone, and sure enough a dynamic duo was formed when he met Crazy Bob from Leeds. If ever two people were destined to upset the Turks, then these two fitted the bill perfectly. Doddy had flown over on a seven-day excursion package with the Turkish national airline, and had met Crazy Bob on that flight. For their first night in Istanbul they decided that a night of abuse of the locals was on the agenda, which would go something like this.

They would walk into a bar and order a drink.

'Oi, Turkface, give us a beer.'

While they drank they would abuse people who spoke no English.

'Is it true all Turks are faggots?'

'Are you a bummer?'

'You look like a bummer.'

The conversation would go on like this all night if trouble didn't break out. The first night they entered a bar and after twenty minutes of non-stop abuse the whole bar erupted and turned on them and they only just made it out of the door. Doddy made me nervous. Crazy Bob petrified me.

The coach for the under-21 match turned up at the hotel and apart from the Chelsea fans a group of other people had turned up. Lenny and Neale were two Arsenal fans whom I had played football against and I tagged along with them for the coach journey to Bursa, which would take about six hours. On the journey Ginger Terry found out I was a keen chess player and challenged me to a game. We crossed the Bosphorus and entered Asia, arriving in Bursa about an hour before kick-off. We bought tickets from the box office, where the Turks gathered round us, chattering noisily and excitedly. A few of us bought Turkish hats and put them on, and this upset a couple of the Chelsea fans.

'Take off those hats. We're England fans,' shouted one.

This really annoyed me because at six feet three inches tall and with ginger hair I don't need to walk around with a flag draped around myself to be recognised as English. I hate dawdling, and as everyone was just hanging around I decided to go on to the terraces on my own. As soon as I entered the ground the Turks spotted me and a small group of them called me over. One of them scurried off and fetched a sheet of cardboard for me to sit on. I was being made guest of honour. The Turks are fanatical about football, but they obviously respected this Englishman coming to their country and sitting on the terrace alongside them.

The ground was small and most of it was terraced. The steps on the terrace were about two feet high, so as the crowd was small everyone was sitting down. Just as the teams came out I saw Hickey and his group enter the seated section above the tunnel where the players enter and leave the field. The army had seen them and taken them into the seats. I felt a bit sick that I was sitting on my own on the terraces. When the Turks noticed the Union Jack with Chelsea written on it, they jeered loudly.

The game was very boring and ultimately finished with no score. But one pathetic incident brought attention to the Chelsea fans: those same racists who had caused such scenes on the South American tour were up to their tricks again. At half- and full-time they made monkey noises and threw bananas at the black players representing England.

There was also the amusing spectacle of young Turks trying to get into the ground without getting caught. One lone security guard had the job of stopping these young urchins from slipping in. The procedure was that if he caught one on the fence in the process of clambering down he ejected them, but if they managed to get on to the terraces he left them alone. Ironically, if he caught one and took him to the gate, another ten would slip in.

After the game the Turks shook my hand warmly and wished me well. Young fans were lighting fires all over the terraces. I decided to make my way round to the seated area where Hickey's group was sitting. The seats were segregated by a big fence so I decided to cut across the pitch which, although it was surrounded by big fences, had gates at the corners, and as most of the crowd had dispersed the groundsman had opened one. I walked down and the head groundsman spotted me and called me over. He was honoured that an Englishman wanted to look at his pitch. I didn't want to, but neither did I want to insult this amiable

Turk. The pitch was in fact extremely bumpy, and the grass very patchy. After going through almost every shot the Turks had played throughout the whole match, the groundsman took me through the players' tunnel and I emerged into the daylight. In front of me was the players' coach, and a policeman, thinking I was an England player, herded me on to the coach where all the under-21 players were sitting like robots in their tracksuits waiting for the manager and officials to get on the coach.

'All right, lads?' I said.

No reply. Everyone just looked at me. I was really annoyed. I had travelled thousands of miles to see this mob play and they couldn't be bothered to say hello to me.

'What's up with you lot, can't you talk?' I sneered at them. I jumped back off the coach extremely indignant that the players hadn't had the decency to speak to me. But in fairness, I didn't know then about the racial chanting and banana throwing that had gone on earlier.

I spotted Hickey's coach and climbed aboard. As we journeyed away from the ground a few young Turks threw stones at the windows, but nothing serious. On the trip back to Istanbul the coach had a refreshment and toilet stop in a small town. I got off and went to get something to eat. When I returned to the coach Lenny, Neale and a group of three others were standing about ten yards away from it. They called me over.

'What do you think about the racist chanting?' one of them asked me.

'What do you mean?' I replied.

He explained to me what had happened at half- and full-time, and I suddenly realised why the England players had ignored me.

'I don't reckon it.'

'It spoils it for everyone. I think someone should have a word with them,' said Lenny

Back on the coach Lenny and I approached a couple of them. The conversation went something, like this.

'Why do you chant at black players?'

' 'Cos they're niggers, ain't they?'

'But surely they are representing England"

'Black players don't count, do they?'

'You *must* cheer when one scores?' (For Chelsea.)

'Nope. I just sit there.'

'What about Paul Cannonville?' (A black Chelsea player.)

'Don't cheer if he scores.'

I found the conversation quite hilarious. We all devised situations where the racists would cheer if a black Chelsea player scored. 'Chelsea are drawing nil–nil in the FA Cup Final against Spurs (Chelsea's greatest rivals), and Paul Cannonville scores. What would you do?'

'I would just sit there, wouldn't I.' We all roared with laughter. The more blatant the racist remarks they came out with, the more we laughed and the more outrageous became our situations. I hoped that in the next day's full international a black player *would* score so that I could observe their reactions.

Racism at football does exist, but apart from the small number of hardcore racists who have attached themselves to certain football clubs, real racism is not as widespread as is often thought. Though some white fans may say 'I hate niggers', almost all will cheer like mad when a black player scores a goal or proves he is a good player. On the terraces, for the most part, everyone is the same colour – that of the team. There is some polarisation: Arsenal, for instance, have black gangs. But I have never seen or heard of racial clashes at football matches. In adversity or triumph, black, white, yellow and brown come together under the club colours to fight or to celebrate. The media are over-sensitive and have considerably exaggerated football racism; and it is significant that the National Front have had very little success recruiting at football.

Once back in Istanbul I decided to catch a taxi down to the ground with Lenny and two others who didn't have tickets, to try to buy some. We pulled up near the ground and as we went to get out a huge gang of young Turks spotted us and ran towards us. I don't think they wanted our autographs, so we all jumped back in and shouted at the driver, 'Drive on.'

He just sat there.

'Drive on!' I screamed.

We were all shouting, gesticulating and even praying for him to drive, but he didn't move until the first youngster banged on his car. He stuck it into gear and revved through them all like a raving madman, scattering young Turks everywhere. As we drove down the road we all breathed a sigh of relief. I looked behind and saw the gang shaking their fists.

We pulled up near the hotel and spotted a restaurant below the level of the pavement. It was our lucky night, for not only was the food superb and cheap but it was opposite the international university and was full of pretty girls. We sat in there all night, talking, drinking and laughing. When I got back to my hotel I saw a group of Chelsea fans sitting at the bar.

'All right, Ginger. Where you been?'

'A little restaurant up the road.'

'I bet the food was shit. Everything's shit in this city.'

'Yeah, something like that,' I replied.

I retired to my room. It would have been pointless trying to put them right, because they would only have abused the place.

The next day I had breakfast in the hotel restaurant and then went into the bar. The match was not until later in the afternoon so a spot of sightseeing was on the cards. A group of four guys were going to the covered bazaar; one of them, Willie Jones, had a stolen Visa card, and he invited me along. The bazaar in Istanbul is quite a sight, and anything can be bought there. Nothing has a price on it so everything has to be bartered for. Willie's eyes lit up when he got to the bazaar. Everywhere accepted Visa cards, and there wasn't a telephone in the place. He went berserk, and he didn't even want to go to the match later in the day. If he had stayed a week he would have owned half of Istanbul!

I was very nervous and kept out of the way, but I had to marvel at his cheek. He was buying gear for everyone and charging nominal fees for the goods: gold, silver, onyx, a replica medieval ball and chain, and leather coats for everyone. In one shop he bought another member of the party a leather coat, and when the Turkish shopkeeper asked him how he would like to pay he replied, 'Visa card, of course. I like to travel with plastic money because there are so many criminals about nowadays.'

We left the bazaar and headed back to the hotel. Willie turned to me.

'Oi; Ginger, you're the only guy who didn't ask for anything in the bazaar. Why's that?'

'Didn't have what I wanted in there.'

'What you after?'

'Rolex Oyster Perpetual.'

'No problem, Ginger, I'll get one up the Sheraton. You pay me twenty per cent of the asking price.'

'You've got a deal,' I said.

Willie walked up the road moaning about how little time he had left in Istanbul and how he could make a fortune in this city. He even thought about flying back a couple of days later and buying up all the gold, but I don't think he had the nerve to smuggle it back on his own. It was noticeable that a big plank of a guy called Al was carrying his gear. Especially heavy was an onyx chess set for Ginger Terry.

The Sheraton Hotel in Istanbul is on top of a hill and overlooks the ground where England were due to play. The England team were staying in the hotel and it was here that I had to pick up my tickets. I made my way up to the hotel about two hours before kick-off with Willie and two other Chelsea fans who were ticketless. Willie went off to buy the Rolex but it fell through because they wanted to check the card, although he did manage to wangle his way out without losing the card. A few England fans were hanging around in the foyer looking for tickets but not having any luck. A desk had been set up and I went and collected my tickets. Ted Croker came into the foyer and a couple of fans approached him for tickets. I heard his reply: 'The match is sold out. There are no spare tickets and the FA will not attempt to get any for you. You've all wasted your journey and it serves you right.'

He looked and sounded so smug, but he didn't realise that getting a ticket abroad is not really a problem. Foreigners don't have the same 'do it right' attitude the British have, and anyway an English five-pound note would be enough to bribe most Turkish gatemen. Two Southampton fans spotted Mark Wright, Southampton's centre-half, and went up to him. Southampton is a small, homely club and after a friendly conversation he disappeared and turned up about ten minutes later with a couple of complimentary tickets. These were red- and gold-edged embossed cards which looked really elegant. I was jealous as hell: what a souvenir to take back to England! They were overjoyed, and we all went back to the bar to celebrate. I spotted Ron Greenwood, the ex-England manager, and walked over to him.

'Hello, Ron,' I said

He totally ignored me and hurried off looking petrified. I found his attitude and that of the other England officials strange. We were not wanted. But I didn't really care, and just before we left the bar to travel the short distance down the hill to the ground Brian Moore, the TV commentator, spoke to us in the bar.

'How's it going, lads?'

'All right, Brian.'

'Being treated fairly by the Turks?'

'No problem from the Turks, it's the pompous FA twits we have to worry about.'

He laughed and we shrugged and left. The trip down the hill took about three minutes and as we got to the ground I noticed the army out in force. We were recognised as English and pushed towards an entrance. We had to walk past a steep wall which formed the back of the terrace containing the Turkish fans. About fifty Turks were screaming things at us, but I don't think it was malicious; they just get so worked up about football. Suddenly a stone was thrown, but no problem because we were soon under cover and out of harm's way. We were being herded by the army through a small turnstile. The officers weren't interested in whether or not we had tickets, they just wanted all the England fans in the same section.

'Look at this, boys,' shouted a voice.

I turned round and saw the England under-21 players coming towards our entrance, and the look on their faces was one of anxiety. Dave Sexton, the team's manager, led the way and walked straight through the crowd. The Chelsea fans made a gangway and shook his hand, for he used to manage Chelsea. He went through, but then as the players followed him the ranks closed. A Chelsea fan turned to them. 'Listen, boys, down here on the streets you are the kiddies and we are the guv'nors, so you wait until we have all gone in. If you lot are so ignorant you won't talk to us, then we won't be polite to you.' Not one of the under-21 players made a move; they just stood there and waited in line. The Turkish army did not seem bothered – as far as they were concerned we were all Englishmen together.

Once inside the ground all the English were being searched, and Dave Sexton was standing by the gate to smooth the passage of the under-21 players. I got to the gate and said, 'Hello Dave, how's it going, mate?'

Dave turned and said to me, 'Where are all the players?'

'Outside, queuing up like polite Englishmen,' I replied.

He looked bemused, and I went on up the steps. Dave is a kindly-looking man, but his attitude, like that of all FA officials, is one of strained toleration towards the supporters.

At the top of the steps I looked out on the ground, which was compact and mostly terraced. The pitch was surrounded by a running track, and we were in the main stand. There were not many England fans present, but they had put us in a small section together. A large contingent of Turkish army senior NCOs sat in the stand on the left. This was obviously the place to sit, and they were not going to be moved by anyone. They all had three stars on the front of their flat-topped peaked caps. Hickey, who was wearing a ridiculous First World War flying cap and goggles, made his way forward with his Chelsea Union Jack and draped it over the front of the stand for the benefit of the TV cameras around the world. He looked back and shouted out, 'I'm in with the three-star generals.'

Most of the seats were taken, but everyone squashed in and I sat on the concrete steps on my newspaper. Ken Bailey was sitting near the front. Ken is an old-age pensioner who travels round the world watching England play sport, and he always dresses up in Union Jack clothes. He is a harmless old man who is living out his last days doing something he enjoys. You get the impression, though, that the FA officials do not like him – possibly because he is more famous than they are.

After taking a few photographs of the crowd, I came back to my spot and struck up a conversation with one of the under-21 players who, I think, was Bradford City's goal-keeper. I asked him if any of the players had been sightseeing in the city, but he told me that they had just stayed in the Sheraton all the time. I found it quite amusing that most of the under-21 players expected us to give up our seats for them simply because they were footballers. The most arrogant player among them was Barry Venison, but Hickey made him look silly at half-time. Hickey walked up the steps and Barry, who had stood the whole time on the steps, barred his way.

'Excuse me,' said Hickey.

'Why, mate, have I got your seat?' enquired Barry.

'No, you plum, we've got your seats. Now get out of the way or else you'll get another terrace lesson.' Barry moved to one side, very red-faced.

England came out and slaughtered the Turks on the football pitch, winning eight–nil. It was a momentous victory, and when John Barnes scored I immediately looked towards the Chelsea racists. Sure enough, they never moved an inch. I meant to ask them their idea of the score of the match later in the hotel, but it slipped my mind. I wished black players had scored all the goals, because that would really have spoilt their day.

In the second half I looked across to the next section and I saw Clive Allen and Remi Moses sitting on the concrete steps looking very glum. The million-pound footballers were having to slum it, and they didn't like it one bit. One of the Chelsea fans shouted over, 'Oi, Clive, want a bit of newspaper to sit on? I would hate the thought of you having to buy a new suit.' The players definitely showed themselves up for what they were; they would do well to remember where they came from.

At the final whistle Salford and Binman both appeared behind us, having previously been spotted at the Turkish end waving the William of Orange flag to screams of abuse by the Turks. We all left together and walked up the hill towards the Sheraton with a large contingent of the army surrounding us. To our left was a huge grassy bank which was quite steep. On the top of the hill was a large group of young Turks who were throwing rocks and bottles at us. This continued until the army charged at them and they scattered. Salford was at the front and charged forward at the Turks who stood in the road in front of us. The Turks ran everywhere, but the army were not happy and one Turkish captain said loudly in English: 'Do not misbehave in Turkey.' I had seen enough of the Turkish army to know that he meant what he said, but there were no more incidents and everyone filed into the Sheraton.

The Istanbul Sheraton is very plush and has a little pond and waterfall in the foyer. It is all marble, and the beer is quite expensive, but everyone just sat around talking and drinking beer. Later, in the early evening, Ray Wilkins the footballer went to sit with the Blackburn group and bought a monster round of drinks. He lives and plays football in Italy, and was pleased to talk to English people while he waited for his plane back there, the rest of the England party having flown back home straight after the game. He was unlike most footballers; I found him quite intelligent and articulate.

There were quite a few people sitting about, and when a small group of Turks appeared outside the glass doors, all hell broke loose. Everyone charged up to the doors; but no one had the bottle to run out and charge into the Turks, and the Turks didn't have the courage to come in. The hotel workers were saying, 'No, no'. A glass was thrown and shattered everywhere on the hotel frontage. One guy snatched open the door and shouted to me, 'I'll hold the door, you go and get them,'

'*I'll* hold the door, *you* go and get them,' I replied.

The Turks ran when two burly barmen charged out and whacked a couple of them. I thought it was quite amusing, but the chap who had held the door didn't see it in the same light.

'They're all wankers,' he said.

'How's that?' I asked.

'Well, if two or three more West Ham had been here then we would have gone out and into them.'

'You had your chance to go out the door and flunked it,' I said.

I found out that this particular guy was called BJ and was reckoned to be a face in a gang called the Under-5s, a group that follows West Ham. He was tall, had dark hair and wore a Burberry anorak. I found him obnoxious, like most West Ham fans. He didn't like me because he realised that I had seen him show fear. Another chap with him seemed quite a reasonable person. Later in the evening the rest of the West Ham fans turned up and after a little sneer at everyone they all left together.

I went upstairs to have a drink in the top-floor bar with a wondrous view of Istanbul, which at night looks quite spectacular. On coming downstairs I bumped into Lenny and Bruce and we had a quick drink in the downstairs bar where we met Brian Glanville, the *Sunday Times* journalist. Usually I haven't much time for newspapermen but I found Brian an exception. He had a passion for Italy and Italian football, and he was certainly very interesting to listen to. I have very strong views on football and I love debating. Brian Glanville is a worthy adversary.

Back at the hotel, Hickey was disappointed that he had missed the one and only row of the trip. We sat in the bar all night talking and telling stories. I listened to some fantastic tales about Salford and Binman. Apparently Binman had lost his trousers in the surf in Rio de Janeiro, and from the stories I heard I felt a little regretful that I had not gone to South America. I turned in at about two in the morning, and on arising at nine I surveyed the carnage in the bar. Some of the guys had been drinking all night and were in a right mess. They were all due to go home that morning and I laughed as they staggered on to the coach.

When they boarded the aeroplane at Istanbul the other people on the plane gave them some very strange looks. It was a KLM plane flying to Amsterdam, and had flown in from Cairo. One of the England fans knew one of the stewardesses on the plane and she told him that before boarding had begun at Istanbul the captain had made a special announcement: 'There is a small contingent of English football hooligans getting on board. Please do not be alarmed by their behaviour or appearance.' No wonder everyone had looked at them like circus animals when they boarded the plane. The irony of it was that no one drank a drop on the trip home, and most of them spent the entire journey in the toilets causing huge queues for the economy-class passengers.

I went and found myself a hotel next to the Pudding Shop and spent an enjoyable day sightseeing. A lot of England fans had booked weekly flights and that Thursday night a lot of us gathered in the Pudding Shop for a drink. Thankfully the West Ham fans had gone to Anatolia for a few days, so it was just good fun. I met some very interesting people, especially a Leyton Orient fan who dressed like an ageing hippie. One guy from Birmingham warned us about walking down by the docks at night, as the first night he had been in Istanbul he had almost had his throat cut. He had been walking along when he had been dragged into an alleyway, had a ten-inch carving knife put next to his throat, and been told, 'Give me your money.' He had had sixty pounds on him and had lost the lot. Later in the evening BJ and his friend came in and I went over to them.

'Want to join us?' I asked.

'No thanks,' replied BJ.

'Why not?'

'Well, I can't be your friend, can I – I might have to give you a kicking when we play Arsenal.'

'That makes you the loser then, because you've got to sit here and stew while we have a good time.'

I could see his friend wanted to join us, but they drank for another thirty minutes and left. The beer flowed that night. But the Pudding Shop was nothing like the place portrayed in *Midnight Express*. In the film it looked atmospheric and romantic, but in reality it was like a transport cafe with plastic chairs and white and brown Formica-topped tables. Being a football fan, though, this doesn't matter, for roughing it on your travels is part of the fun. Watching football and the excitement generated at venues all around the world is great, though it really cheeses you off when you travel halfway across the globe and England players and officials just turn their backs on you. After all, a few polite words and a smile cost nothing. We spoke at length about this in the Pudding Shop that night.

Friday came and a boat excursion was planned across the Bosphorus. As we cruised over to Asia I looked back on the walled city and imagined what it must have looked like hundreds of years ago. I felt sorry that the England players had not had the chance to see such a wonderful sight. In today's climate the win-at-all-costs mentality has deprived footballers of the chance to savour the delights of foreign travel. Most of them are young men with little or no experience of life, and for some of the under-21 players who will not make the grade, the chance to see Istanbul may have been lost for ever. To travel all the way to Turkey and remain in the Sheraton seems an appalling waste of an opportunity.

Friday night saw us create a huge party in the Sultan pub, which was just like a British public house complete with a stereo system on which the owner played English music. We got all the Turks singing and dancing. The army waited outside, and huge crowds peered in through the windows. Doddy nearly started a riot by upsetting the Turks with Crazy Bob, but it was soon smoothed over. A few Sudanese guest workers were in the bar and they thought it was great fun to join in the dancing. As celebrations go I think this was the best I have ever participated in.

After Friday, Saturday night was bound to be an anti-climax, but when I saw the group of West Ham fans at about 7.00 p.m. I knew that trouble would ensue. I got into the Sultan at about 7.30, and everyone was in there. The owner welcomed me and wanted to know what time the dancing would start. The West Ham fans, about seven of them including BJ, sat at the far end next to the exit to the toilets. They were abusing everyone, especially the Leyton Orient fan who after ten minutes got up and left. I went round a few people to see if anyone was prepared to fight them, but no one had the courage. One of them, called Danny, had some eggs which he threw at me. I went over and told him to pack it in, but they just laughed. It was embarrassing, especially as the happy atmosphere of the pub changed to one of trepidation. The two Sudanese guys who had been in the pub the night before were dancing around and shaking everyone's hand. But they made the mistake of trying to shake the ginger-haired West Ham fan's hand.

'Piss off, nigger,' he said.

The Sudanese guy was stopped in his tracks, but tried again to be friendly.

'Piss off, nigger,' said Danny.

One of the others punched him quite hard and cut his lip. The owner of the bar came over and quickly restored calm. The Turks are not too keen on the Sudanese, but the owner didn't want any trouble and he had seen the egg throwing. He spoke to me.

'Sort out your friends.'

'They are no friends of mine.'

'They are English, aren't they?'

'Well, yes, but they're the scumbags of England.'

The ginger-haired guy overheard my conversation and walked over. 'What's your game?' he asked.

'What do you mean?' I replied.

'Talking about English people like that.'

I grabbed hold of his lapels and he began yelling 'Let go of my coat.' I held on, but he went crazy. 'Get your hands off me!' he shouted.

He didn't frighten me, and despite the fact that I could only have improved his looks by thumping him I was wary of his mates, so I let go. But I was determined to give him a piece of my mind.

'Now listen here, we have been well liked and respected by everyone in this bar but you lot of slags have spoilt it by your pathetic behaviour. You should be ashamed of yourselves.'

He had no answer and simply told me, with great originality, to 'fuck off', then walked away. I went and sat down with a few other people I had met the previous night. The thing that annoyed me the most was the fact that they would not have done a thing if the Chelsea fans had been in the bar. But now Doddy and Crazy Bob were drinking with them, and the dynamic duo were taking great delight in abusing the Sudanese.

Their final act of moronic behaviour was reserved for two young English girls who had run out of money and were travelling back to England. There was a lorry park just outside Istanbul and they needed money to get out there and back each day to try to hitch a lift back to Munich. I saw the way Turkish men looked at English women and realised why they needed to be able to refuse lifts if they felt the driver was a bit dodgy. One of the girls was selling her camera and other gear. A whip-round was organised for the girls and a reasonable sum of money was raised. One of the West Ham fans came over with a small sum of Turkish money. 'This is for you if you do me a blow job, luv,' he said to one of the girls. It was disgusting and I felt ashamed. The girl told him to clear off, but his friends thought it was great.

This, unfortunately, is the mentality of many English football fans abroad. They left shortly afterwards and got involved in a punch-up outside the Pudding Shop. Saturday night in Istanbul is not the place to have a punch-up, and they soon found about fifty Turks coming at them. The West Ham fans and Doddy ran for dear life, leaving Crazy Bob to take a fearful beating. He came back into the Sultan well battered and bruised, but luckily nothing was broken. Bob and I decided to take a taxi back to Doddy's hotel, and we shook hands with the owner. I gave him my England hat to put above the bar and we went to the door. Unfortunately, the Turks who had beaten up Crazy Bob were waiting outside. We decided to make a dash for the taxi rank and shout 'Airport!' once inside a taxi. The door opened and out we shot – a quick sprint across the road and into a taxi. 'Airport, pronto!' I shouted. He sped off, but two hundred yards up the road and with the danger passed we gave him the card of the hotel and, looking slightly bemused, he drove there.

Doddy was sitting in the bar of the hotel still shaking from the punch-up, even though he had neither thrown a punch nor received one. Within half an hour, though, he was back to normal and was abusing the hotel waiter. We shared a taxi back to the airport but I wished I hadn't when Doddy, sitting in the front seat, kept grabbing the steering wheel causing the taxi to swerve, and Crazy Bob kept sticking his smelly feet right under the taxi driver's nose. As we were sorting out the fare at the airport Doddy and Bob started abusing the poor taxi driver and disputing the fare. Another Turk who intervened to try to help and reason with Bob ended up with a bloody nose, courtesy of a Crazy Bob head-butt. 'Now butt out, Turk face!' shouted Bob, then paid the fare in full and even gave a tip.

We walked into the airport. I had three hours to wait for my plane; Bob and Doddy had seven. We went into the buffet and there met a real character. Frankie was sitting in the buffet drinking beer, but was not drunk. He was alone, and his first words were: 'What do you think of Istanbul whores?' We explained that none of us had tried them. He was absolutely appalled. 'It is the duty of every Englishman to sample the whores in every city where England plays football.'

I found him very amusing and good value for a three-hour waiting period at an airport, pretty boring at the best of times. Frankie came from Luton and had just flown back from Ankara where, it seemed, he had found the whores far superior to those in Istanbul. We sat around a table talking for two hours about the relative merits of prostitutes the world over although we didn't talk so much as listen to Frankie. He was very proud of his passport stamps because each had its own particular story. He was enthusiastic about Copenhagen and ecstatic about Rio de Janeiro. I wondered where he got his money, and he told me he had inherited a large sum at the age of twenty-one. I couldn't fault the guy. This was his hobby, however bizarre it might seem to you and me. His final words to me as I left the buffet to go to the gate for my plane were: 'I have got standards, you know. I always give the girls a tip when England win!'

I didn't stop laughing to myself all the way back to England. Turkey had been great fun, but the old cliché had been proven: it takes only a few people to spoil all the good done by the majority.

The only other away game I fancied in our group was in Northern Ireland. I knew that the Northern Irish fans liked a punch-up, because at their previous meeting Hickey and a few others had been set upon and Hickey had taken quite a beating. I phoned him a couple of weeks before the match and he told me he had a coach leaving on the Tuesday night and returning to London Thursday evening. We would be in Belfast for Wednesday at 11 a.m. and would only have to miss two working days. Everybody met up in the Black Bull at about six Tuesday evening. Doddy was in the pub and he greeted me like a long-lost friend. He promised me faithfully he wouldn't abuse any Paddies, but I didn't believe a word of it.

Hickey's coach was not full and it was a pretty old-looking thing. The driver was covered in grease and oil and he looked as if he had been repairing it to get it on the road. The route we were due to take was via Holyhead and Dublin. The coach party consisted mostly of Chelsea fans but, as on the Turkey trip, a large cross-section of other fans was also on board. The coach had to stop in Kilburn, north London to pick up Salford. To him the trip to Northern Ireland was a religious exercise. He was looking forward to a trip up the Shankill Road, the stronghold of the Protestants in Belfast. A couple of younger guys at the back of the coach had a lot of National Front literature which I read, but they expressed dismay that I didn't support the Front or its views on repatriation. A large Union Jack which had Chelsea written in white letters across the centre was hung at the back of the coach. A couple more Union Jacks were hung across the windows, just to let everyone know who we were.

A beer stop was made at an off-licence in north London where Hickey informed everyone that if they must steal beer then they should be discreet because we had a ferry connection at Holyhead and had no time to spare. The coach also stopped on a motorway somewhere to pick up a man called Mark, who came from Nottingham. He boarded the coach with a carrier bag full of National Front literature. He wanted to show his loyalist brothers in Northern Ireland that certain political parties would not give in to the cowardly IRA – or at least, that's how he put it.

There wasn't much beer drunk. It was like a day trip to the seaside with lots of sixties Beatles songs being sung. Hickey sat at the front of the coach like a schoolmaster, taking requests for the video screen. One of the guys had put together a video of all the news clips he had seen on football violence. It made for interesting viewing, and the clip of trouble in Copenhagen was made even more appropriate by one of the coach party recognising himself getting a punch in the mouth from a policeman.

The only incident occurred in a cafeteria at Holyhead, when two brothers who were having a family feud decided to have a punchup and a seat got broken. The woman in the cafeteria made such a fuss that you'd have thought it was World War Three, but there was no real damage so off we went, with the brothers still arguing.

The next morning we docked in Dublin, where we drove through customs without getting stopped at all. About an hour out of Dublin the coach broke down. The driver had come prepared and unloaded a toolbox and set to work on the engine. All we could do was sit and watch, but a couple of guys took the opportunity to clean the back window so that everybody could see that we were Chelsea fans. After about forty minutes the driver got back in and started up the coach. A huge cheer went up and we were on our way again. On the drive to Belfast, and even at the border crossing, the army presence was minimal. The countryside was lovely, hard to equate with the images one has of Northern Ireland from the TV news.

Upon arrival in Belfast the coach dropped us outside the Europa hotel, which is done up like a fortress because it has been bombed so many times. Some of the people on the coach explained that on the previous trip the army had manned checkpoints into the town centre, but now the security situation had eased and although the checkpoints were still there they were unmanned. A pub opposite the Europa called Robinsons was named as the meeting place where the coach would pick us up at midnight after the match.

Within half an hour of us arriving in Belfast, Mark, the National Front guy, had been pulled in by the Royal Ulster Constabulary for distributing his literature. The RUC confiscated all his material and told everyone that the wearing of NF badges would not be allowed in pubs in this part of town. Salford, who had travelled to this game without Binman (who had come by train on the Stranraer–Larne route), made his way up to the Orange Cross Club, a strong Protestant club which made no bones about what it stood for. When you walked in it had military decorations and pictures of the Queen everywhere. Pride of place went to a Victoria Cross won by a member of the club in the First World War.

One of the guys on the trip told me that although all the people at the match supporting Northern Ireland would be staunch loyalists, this would not prevent them from giving you a punch in the mouth after the game. The previous time England had played in Belfast the police had simply left the England fans to make their own way back to the station, and all the Paddies had come out of the pubs for a good punch-up. This didn't bother me as much as the fact that nobody on our coach had match tickets and the match had been sold out for two weeks. The newspapers were saying that nobody would gain entry without a ticket and to not even bother turning up as it was a pointless exercise. I felt confident because most of the other people on our coach didn't seem worried about getting tickets. We had all heard the 'sold out, won't gain entry' business bandied about before.

I went for a drink in the Orange Cross Club, which from the outside looked pretty drab. It had an Orange Cross hanging on a flagpole, representing the Battle of the Boyne. Nobody was inside and I found out that everyone was drinking further up the road. I finally found most of the guys and even managed to have a sensible drink with Doddy, which

must go down in history. The Irish were very friendly, especially as they saw our coming as a vindication of the strength
of the Unionists. I was determined to go down the Falls
Road, the staunchly Catholic area of Belfast, and asked what
my chances were of walking down there. I was warned off
that, but as no buses went there I decided to take a taxi as far
as the army barracks. I found another England fan who
wanted to see a bit more than just the inside of a Protestant
club, so off we went. An old Protestant told us: 'I wouldn't
give the Fenian bastard taxi drivers one penny to take me
down the Falls.'

We had been told that it would be difficult to get a taxi
down the Falls, but the first taxi driver we came across was
only too willing. The other England fan who accompanied
me was named Raymond and was just twenty-one years old.
All he had with him was a carrier bag with his Union Jack in.
I hoped the taxi wouldn't break down because I didn't fancy
a walk back up the Falls with a Union Jack.

The journey was quite interesting. Belfast seemed just
like any other city, apart from the paintings on the walls.
There was one which showed the sign representing the
female species, and in the centre was a picture of an Arab
female, an African female and an Irish female. It was a
huge picture in black and white and took up the whole
side of a house. Next to it were the words 'Cowardly
Loyalist Backout'. The murals were very impressive, and
almost all depicted the struggle for freedom. It was a total
contrast to the loyalist paintings on the sides of the houses
on the Shankill estates, which depicted solidarity with the
mainland. The army barracks at the bottom of the Falls
was an incredible sight. It had huge smooth walls which
pointed outwards at the top – to stop mortar attacks, I
think. It must be horrible being inside, rather like being in
prison.

We cruised back to Robinsons bar feeling rather pleased

with ourselves. Once inside I spotted my old friends the West Ham fans. They were all there – BJ, Danny and Taffy to name but a few. My old ginger mate from Istanbul was there, but he ignored me. Danny said an arrogant 'Hello' in a voice which informed that he was in charge. Thankfully they left shortly afterwards. We settled in for the afternoon drink and most England fans were congregating down there. At about 4.30 in the afternoon a group from our coach decided to go for a walk up the Falls Road, but they didn't get very far before the army and RUC turned them back.

The Irish seemed quite friendly. I spoke to a few and they all had tickets but seemed very sure we wouldn't be able to get any. I decided, along with a few friends, to make my way down to the ground at about 6.30. When I got to the bar I saw that a large contingent of RUC had gathered outside to pre-empt any trouble that might break out. They all carried big truncheons and sten guns. The walk to the ground took about twenty-five minutes, and once outside we all stood asking people for any spare tickets. One young Irishman came over and I asked him if he had a ticket. He replied, 'I would rather burn it than give it to an Englishman.'

At that point the West Ham fans turned up and started a huge punch-up with some Paddies. The Paddies were well game and it became a stand-off situation. Just as I was hopeful of getting a ticket, the RUC moved me on. An Irishman came up and told me that tickets were being sold in the street over the bridge behind the ground. I was getting pretty desperate by now. I went over the bridge, but all the England fans I met told me that they were having no luck. I was standing in a big car-park asking everyone, and all of a sudden an Irishman approached me. 'Looking for a ticket?' he asked.

'Yeah. How much?'

'Face value, I don't want to make a profit,' he replied. I laughed at all the English press who had quoted official sources as saying, 'Don't bother turning up without a ticket.' I never saw anybody fail to get a ticket that night, although some did bribe the gatemen instead. Even the West Ham fans got in. Once inside I stood to the left rather than behind the goal with the rest of the England fans.

The match was won by England one–nil and at the end the Irish filed out while the RUC stood in a line to stop any England fans leaving. They decided to give them an escort back to the station. The young Irish fans were walking right up to the lines to try to have a swing at the English, and the RUC practically had to punch them to get them to back off. There were about five of us standing alone on the terraces. I decided to walk outside to have a look at the car-park, but as I got to the exit I saw a huge mob of Irish waiting for us. I came back in and saw Ginger Terry. I told him what I had seen but he just shrugged his shoulders. 'I expect it'll be a big punch-up, like last time,' he said.

After about ten minutes the stadium was cleared and Ginger Terry was talking to an Irishman who had lived a long time in Kilburn. Another big Irishman walked into the stadium and spoke to him: 'Are we going to have a go at the English or not?'

'I'm not,' he replied. 'But they're all there, so if you want to feel free.'

The big Irishman scowled and walked out of the ground and back into the car-park. Five minutes later the RUC began to beckon the English fans forward. The West Ham fans took pole position. I took up residence in the middle, trying to spot any of the group I had travelled with. The walk back to our pick-up point took us through a labyrinth of dark back streets with terraced houses on each side. The Irish had no fear of us, and they had no fear of arrest. They stood around the streets just waiting for the punch-up. The

West Ham fans at the front were fighting all and sundry, along with Hickey and his group.

Suddenly I saw the huge Irishman whom I had seen enter the ground earlier standing on the pavement. He was wearing a Linfield FC jumper. 'I'll fight the best Englishman amongst you,' he said. I hit him with an absolute beauty which rocked him on his heels. I hit him again and again. He reeled back and I kicked him once. The next thing I knew I was being dragged backwards with a truncheon across my throat by three RUC officers. They threw me up against the armoured Land Rover. One of the officers hit me across the back with his truncheon, and it hurt. The sergeant gripped me round the throat. 'If I see you blink, I will lock you up for the night.' He pushed me away from the Land Rover and I walked back to the pavement. I was pleased to get away with that one, for I didn't fancy missing Hickey's coach back to Dublin.

As soon as I got round the corner I received a punch in the mouth from another Paddy. I didn't hit him back as I didn't want to get arrested. The RUC were all around and told us to stop where we were on a bridge. The Irish stood on the other side of the road. A group of Geordies, who had been involved in the fight alongside the West Ham and had seen me get pulled up by the RUC, struck up a conversation with me.

'What did the RUC say?' one asked me.

'Just threatened me with arrest,' I replied.

'Are you West Ham?'

'No, I'm Arsenal.'

'Those West Ham are well game.'

Our conversation was interrupted by a group of Irish across the road taunting us.

'If it wasn't for the coppers, you'd be mincemeat.'

'I think you live in dreamland, Paddy,' replied one of the Geordies.

The RUC tried to move the Irish on, but they just ignored them. I presume that arrests are kept to the minimum because they haven't time to go to court for such trivial matters. We stood on the bridge for no apparent reason, but in the distance we heard a bang. A bomb had exploded. The sound chilled our bones. We moved off, with the Irish following us at a discreet distance. I felt good now with the Geordies, because I knew they could handle themselves. A group of three British Army armoured cars sped past and a loud cheer went up from the English football fans.

At a fork in the road with a large pub on the right the bulk of the fans went off with the escort towards the station. The Geordies went with them, while our group walked back down the road to the Europa hotel. We had only about four RUC men with us and one armoured land Rover. A group of Irish fans was standing outside the pub, shouting, 'Come back, you English cowards, and fight like men.' The sound rang in our ears as we walked down the road. Three Irishmen were following just behind, taunting us and casting doubt on the legitimacy of our birth.

Just as we got to Robinsons bar the West Ham fans spotted them and ran for them, but the RUC intervened. I walked across the road with big Ralph, a giant of a guy, who was on Hickey's coach. We waited on the corner expecting the Irish to walk away, but to our surprise they walked over and called us cowards. The punches rained on them thick and fast, and I particularly enjoyed punching the big-mouth. Ralph was incensed, and also punched the big-mouth as he tried to run away. Unfortunately Ralph was still thumping him when the RUC turned up, and he got himself arrested and thrown into the back of a Land Rover. The West Ham fans were ignored although they were still knocking the hell out of the other Irishmen. I bet that was the last time those Paddies called a group of Englishmen cowards.

The RUC wanted us off the streets, but it was only 10.15 and our coach wasn't due until midnight. The senior RUC man negotiated with the Europa hotel to let us in for a drink, but people began to drift up the road. A couple of guys got Ralph released from the Land Rover, and we walked back up the road towards the pub where we had been called English cowards. However, we didn't get that far as another bar was spotted down a side street. We all filed in and played pool and drank beer until closing time. People were filing in, and one guy appeared with a juicy back eye. He had no scarf on, but he had fallen for the classic ruse.

'What's the time, mate?' the Paddy had asked him.

He hadn't replied but had got a punch in the face for his trouble.

It was an enjoyable evening out, but I was glad when we got on our coach. The Paddies are a tough crowd, and they take no prisoners. The coach journey home was pretty uneventful except for the two young National Front guys sniffing amyl nitrate and offering me some. What it did for them I do not know. I think I'll stick to Vitamin C. To cap it all the coach broke down on the M1 just outside London and everyone got off and left the coach driver to it. So that was it. Another eventful away trip with Hickey was over.

England matches away are much more fun than home games, mostly because of the camaraderie among the people who travel. Sometimes, though, it is upsetting to see the hooligans besmirching the name of England. Young fans in other countries have copied the English hooligans, and now every major city boasts its own 'crew' or 'firm' who follow their team, which can make it very awkward for England fans abroad. With everyone fired up on a heady cocktail of jingoism and booze, it is hard to see how the fighting between home countries' hooligans and our own can be prevented. After all, a country that has as its best-selling newspaper one that glories in the death of 300 sailors with the heading 'GOTCHA' has only itself to blame if it is breeding a nation of delinquents.

8

Colleagues and Adversaries

Football stadiums are full of outrageous people who can be witty, funny and tough. Some are very violent, but these are looked upon by everybody with a certain amount of fear. Nobody wants to get too friendly with that type; after all, who wants to be friends with someone who enjoys hurting people? One character who was certainly larger than life was Hickey. He was known at every football ground in the country and his reputation secured him folk-hero status. Once at Bristol he was confronted by a gorilla of a man who wanted to punch him in the head.

'I'm looking for Hickey, Chelsea's leader.'

'Well, you've found him.'

'Don't be silly, you can't be Hickey. He's big and hard.'

His reputation had preceded him, and this was to prove his undoing. He loved to play the game of terrace fighting. It was just that he was still living in the 1970s while, unfortunately for him, the police were not. The days of a ten-pound fine for disturbing the peace are long gone.

Every time Hickey went to an England away match he

made friends with other fans, and once he had become friends with someone he never fought with them at football. I remember a young Chelsea fan being disillusioned at the sight of Hickey running for his life at Portsmouth. But you don't survive as long as Hickey without running from time to time. Hickey, as everyone knew, was a supreme organiser of coaches. He spoke with an outrageous vocabulary, but a vicious thug – no, never. Because of his reputation, people liked to be seen with him; if he said hello to you it gave you credibility. Every club had its celebrities and the Chelsea group who travelled around the world watching England numbered among them many amusing characters – but none who could hold centre stage like Hickey. He worked as a roadie for a comedian and a stripper who worked the 'stag night' circuit. It was a seedy world of one-night stands in smoke-filled rooms. One night in south London he walked into a club filled with Millwall's Bushwackers. He talked his way out of a beating somehow, but living under constant threat was a hazard of being a known face in the terrace world.

On one occasion I attended a nightclub with a well-known Chelsea guy called Porkys, an overweight fan renowned for his ability to thieve from pub fruit machines. The doorman was a known member of West Ham's Inter City Firm (ICF) and he laughed at Porkys, telling him he was going to punch his lights out when West Ham met Chelsea. The banter was light-hearted, the subject deadly serious. But that was the way it was for most of them: a game to be played on a Saturday – although I do know of incidents where individuals have been attacked in their local pub in mid-week raids. West Ham once made a famous mid-week attack on a 'Gooners' pub in Hackney, where cricket stumps, axes and CS gas were used as weapons. But basically there is a code of honour.

Football is the ideal partisan sport because of the tremendous feelings of identity that the game can offer. When people go to football matches the sense of belonging is incredibly strong. The sheer emotion and ecstasy when a goal is scored lead you to hug and dance with the guy next to you even if you have never met or spoken with him before. The best celebration I ever had was on the banks of the River Trent after a momentous Cup win at Nottingham, when eight people who didn't know each other and have never met since danced a five-minute reel. You can't explain it. It's something you just have to experience.

Hickey was arrested along with Ginger Terry and others on the Thursday before Easter in 1986. It was two days before the annual punch-up between Chelsea and West Ham at Stamford Bridge. I saw the report on the news on Thursday night at the local leisure centre. The police put on display a series of weapons, and it made me laugh to see the imitation medieval ball and chain that I had originally intended to buy from Ginger Terry in Istanbul. The police made out that this was a football terrace weapon. What a load of garbage! Hickey's hobby was collecting imitation medieval weapons. The police activity was called 'Operation Own Goal' and a news team was invited along to film it. So much for the pretext that you are innocent until proven guilty. That seems to apply to everyone except football fans.

The tide, though, had been turning against football hooligans for a long time, and the final straw was the Heysel disaster. After this tragedy the need to secure convictions against football hooligans was given priority by the Thatcher Government to save face. In fact, the Minister for Sport had been warning the Belgian authorities about the possibility of crowd trouble between Italians and English weeks beforehand. He had also asked for strict segregation. The Heysel stadium had been a shambles in 1980. God knows how much it had deteriorated by 1985. As soon as Mrs Thatcher felt that she had been humiliated by football hooliganism, Neil McFarlane (Minister for Sport at the time) was told to shut up and toe the party line, and the Prime Minister set up her 'War Cabinet', or so the tabloid press dubbed it. They wanted convictions against Liverpool fans at first, and after that convictions against hooligans generally. This became even more important after an indefinite ban from European club competition.

The big problem for the hooligans was the fact that they had become known faces, and Hickey especially had become very careless. He would let any Tom, Dick or Harry on his coach. If you had money and liked a drink, then clamber aboard. It was bums on seats: the profit motive. They didn't even have to be able to have a punch-up; there were always plenty of nutters on board who could fight – not that they always came out on top.

Glynn from Leatherhead went on one of Hickey's outings up north and they were ambushed by a load of Wolves fans at a service station on the M1. Hickey and the boys were more than holding their own, but Glynn got separated. He was held down and hit across the spine with a machete. After being taken to a local hospital he was transferred to a special spinal unit, where he was told he could be paralysed for the rest of his life. Miraculously, he regained complete use of everything after a week.

Everybody was sitting in Stamford Bridge's West Stand at half-time talking about the big game in a fortnight's time. It was West Ham at home and the Chelsea men were planning their tactics and trying to work out the West Ham ICF's route to the ground. The loudspeakers around the ground were playing pop music and a disc jockey was announcing requests and introducing the records. The DJ's voice came over the loudspeaker: 'I have a special request here from a Bill Gardener from West Ham. He says hello to Stephen Hickmott, Danny Harkins . . .' The disc jockey went on to name all the known Chelsea faces, and the message went on to say: 'I haven't been to the Bridge for twelve months but I do hope you will reserve a special welcome for me. I hope it's better than the welcome you gave me last year. That was very disappointing.' Everybody turned round and looked at each other in stunned silence.

Up until the death of an Arsenal fan in 1982 I don't think the police or media had heard of the ICF or understood the set-up of the gangs that followed football teams. Arsenal had the Gooners, Spurs the Yiddos, Millwall the Bushwackers and West Ham had the ICF and Under-5s. Chelsea, who never had a named gang, suddenly started calling themselves the Headhunters and even copied the West Ham trick of leaving a calling card on their victims, although I don't think this practice was as widespread as the media made it out to be. Other teams also had gangs with fancy names and titles: Leeds Service Crew, for instance, and, the silliest of all, the Birmingham Zulu Warriors.

All the police had to do was observe the crowds at football matches and build up a dossier on the leaders and faces. With the hooligans' feelings of power and general invincibility it was not difficult, and the decrease in crowds also made the police job much easier. Chelsea and Hickey were picked on, in my opinion, because of their high profile around the world at England games. There was even talk that the National Front sponsored foreign trips to help spread the doctrine. If that had been true then I would certainly have known about it.

The last time I had a drink and a chat with Hickey was on a Wednesday dinner-time at the start of the 1986–87 season. I popped into the Black Bull public house in Chelsea where I knew a few people would be having a drink because Chelsea were playing Leicester later that evening, and this pub was always used as the meeting place for away matches. I warned Hickey that he would have to be very careful after the Heysel tragedy because the police and politicians were sure to have a clamp-down. 'The police don't know where the next punch-up is coming from,' shouted Hickey in his own inimitable way. But it was famous last words, because shortly afterwards two young plain-clothes constables turned up in the pub and began the practice of travelling to the matches on Hickey's coach. It was easy for them, because anyone who turned up was immediately accepted.

After Hickey was arrested, his trial, when it came, was predictable and rested on how much the jury believed what the two police officers said they had seen happen. Nobody believed the police had a case, but Ginger Terry, for all his brains, had kept a diary which seemed to corroborate the constables' evidence. The police made out that Hickey was Terry Last's lieutenant, although I certainly never saw it that way; if anything it was the other way round. I consider the ten-year sentences they both received very harsh, especially when you compare them with rapists' sentences. They never beat up any old women or children. It was just that society needed scapegoats to carry the can. British justice triumphs again!

Furthermore, the much-publicised collapse of all subsequent hooligan trials involving the police must cast doubt on the fairness of Hickmott's and Last's convictions.

I have met people at football matches who became and have remained my friends for life. It forges a bond between you and you discover something about yourself and your fellow men when, on a cold November night in a dingy back street, you are confronted by superior numbers of rival fans coming at you. You learn more about the whole spectrum of human emotions in one split second than you would on a five-year psychology course. Politicians and people who haven't experienced the thrill of football do not understand what makes a hooligan tick, but if any one of those people who condemn people who fight at football could experience the feeling then perhaps they would begin to understand.

It is said that the brain can create its own drug to beat any of the most powerful opiates. If a substance could be created to give that feeling, it would be called an ecstasy pill. I remember once I saw a hooligan interviewed on TV and the smug interviewer asked him why he did it. The hooligan summed it up perfectly, but in a way which left no one any the wiser. 'Yeah, well, it's like this. It's a great feeling going down the terrace with a few hundred behind you making a few hundred back off.'

Some observers say that people who are nobodies in everyday life become somebodies at football. And why should that surprise them? The Thatcher Government in 1987 was elected with only 42 per cent of the popular vote, but I don't see them giving many concessions back to the majority; so is it not understandable that a football hooligan should want to enjoy his bit of power? Most people are nobodies wanting to become somebodies. When some of the hooligans read about the appalling havoc and destruction they have wreaked upon towns and cities, they feel important. In their everyday lives they may not have a particular talent, but on a Saturday they can use their powers of leadership and courage and earn respect. Politicians wring their hands in horror, saying things like, 'Why don't they channel their energies constructively?' – but then omit to tell us where such channels exist for these people. Even when they are in prison, and therefore under the direct control of the authorities, they are not offered much in the way of educational or self-improvement facilities.

The present era of football hooliganism would appear to be coming to an end – at least the visible violence inside the grounds which erupted in the late sixties and reached its zenith in the seventies. The twenty-year span of the phenomenon has seen many different phases. The use of video cameras, the decrease in crowds and the huge numbers and better organisation of the police now make it impossible to have a punch-up and remain anonymous, which has always been so important to the hooligan. The early outbreaks of violence were totally connected with the match itself – a goal being scored or a penalty award – and the threat of violence existed only inside the ground or in its immediate vicinity. Now, though, it seems that violence can erupt anywhere, and people are often attacked up to three hours before or after a match. It has become organised gang violence, with tactics and weapons entering the picture, and the fast attack mentality prevails: get in fast, do the damage and get out again. The grounds have become like caged fortresses, and although the police tactics are generally good, all they seem to have achieved is to transfer the violence elsewhere.

When I was a young man, getting punched in the mouth at football seemed just a part of growing up. There were definitely more fights on the terraces in the 1970s than there are now, but as the match punch-ups have declined, so the violence has moved on and become more serious. There is increasing use of knives in football violence. There were isolated stabbings at matches when I was in my teens, but the carrying of a knife was a rarity; it was considered almost unmanly. Now it seems that every confrontation ends in a stabbing, and that is pretty frightening.

Everyone has their own theories, but the fact is that football is simply a mirror reflection of society – at least, that's certainly true of this country. The level of violence in our society, whatever its cause, has been reflected at football matches for the last twenty years. Football has been seen as an ideal vehicle by groups of young adolescents wanting to express themselves, and they consider their behaviour perfectly normal and acceptable. Football fans, like every other group of people, are only conforming to the practices of their own group. It is similar to upper-class public school-boys playing polo, or young debutantes attending coming-out balls. Politicians throw up their hands in horror at hooliganism, yet consider the way they themselves behave in the House of Commons: so-called civilised people verbally abusing, chanting at, obstructing, interrupting and even occasionally physically assaulting each other. It sounds very much like a football crowd to me. And at least football crowds applaud the opposition sometimes!

I look back on my time on the terraces as an apprentice-ship, part of the learning process, but just as children tend to grow out of asthma, so I grew out of my youthful behaviour. Some people don't however, and the use of weapons in football violence now by men in their late twenties and early thirties (some who are parents themselves) is a frightening fact of life. When the police catch these knife-wielding thugs, young or old, I believe they should be locked up for a long time.

9

Europe '88

While violence inside British grounds is diminishing, a worrying trend is the escalation of bad behaviour at European matches. Young men with no respect for anything see Europe as a gigantic target for abuse. Its diversity of countries and national customs mean nothing; it's simply us (England) and them (foreigners). The football itself is just a good excuse to travel and run amok without fear of being jailed for long periods. I once heard this drunken comment in a Paris bar: 'If the good Lord didn't want us to behave differently to the rest of Europe, then why did he create the English Channel?' That just about sums it up.

Since the 1982 World Cup, the general behaviour and mentality of travelling football fans has deteriorated (and it wasn't all that good before then!) – but there again, so has the general behaviour of young Englishmen in foreign holiday locations. The real worry is that there seems to be no way of stopping trouble, short of mobilising whole armies in whatever country England are playing, or withdrawing passports en masse.

'The party's in Europe,' said Kas Pennant, prominent face
in West Ham's ICF, on a London Weekend Television inter-
view on football violence. A lot of fans see it that way. If it's
a game in Europe within a reasonable distance, then it's a
hooligans' excursion. This was certainly how the majority
saw the 1988 European Championships: a chance to clash
with the hooligans of Germany and Holland. According to
the tabloid press, the Dutch hooligans wanted to match
themselves against the English. A huge security operation
and ticket vetting were launched by the English Football
Association and police, but it didn't stop thousands travelling without tickets. As it turned out, the worst violence
occurred between the Dutch and German fans. Not everyone
who travelled was a hooligan but, unfortunately, the genuine
fans were outnumbered at least 70–30 by the bad-news
'booze brigade'. There was some trouble at the
Championships involving English fans but not on the scale
the English newspapers had predicted. There was not too
much fighting, certainly none in the stadiums, but the booze
culture gives the politicians the chance they have been waiting for to hammer football and introduce a membership card
scheme.

There was always going to be drunken English behav-
iour in Germany. Most of the England fans travelling saw
themselves as a sort of reincarnation of Winston Churchill.
'We'll show the Krauts why they lost the last war' was heard
on a cross-Channel ferry; and 'Two world wars and one
World Cup, doodah, doodah' to the tune of 'Camptown
Races', was sung in most bars during the Championships.
Most people were going to Germany to get drunk, sing
'God Save the Queen', remind the Germans about the last
war, and watch England win the football – in that order.
Any other outcome was therefore impossible, especially
after the hype that had been manufactured by the English
press about the probability of England winning the Cup. To

read the newspapers you would have thought we only had to turn up to win.

Another factor was the common British misconception about foreigners, especially Germans. One England fan was overheard to say, in a Dusseldorf bar, 'All Germans are humourless, sausage-eating squareheads.' There are many similar quotes that illustrate the overall feeling of superiority to people from across the Channel, which leads to a lot of bad behaviour by English football fans. You only have to look at the insularity of many English people abroad. They do not travel to see foreign countries and customs; they merely transfer England and their Englishness somewhere else. They travel en masse to destinations where English food and pubs abound; the only difference is the twenty-four-hour drinking.

This is exactly what happened in Germany: scores of young men who normally invade Spain or Greece descended on Germany and had a good time drinking and being jingoish. The British tabloids and even some of the serious newspapers had a field day. A friend of mine was in a Stuttgart bar having a quiet drink when a reporter entered and said he needed a picture and some quotes for the folks back home. An impromptu conga and an accidentally knocked-over table were translated into a glass-throwing episode for the 'folks back home'. Rumour has it that certain reporters completely manufactured incidents for consumption on the home front. The rest is history, as the saying goes. The Official EUFA report stressed that the trouble was no worse than any average Saturday during the German Football League season. But the politicians didn't want to hear that, because the decision had been made to introduce membership cards, and the exaggerated press hysteria about violence in Germany was the excuse they required.

There may not have been much violence in Germany but the boorish drunken behaviour by travelling England fans did not endear them to the majority of bar owners, hoteliers and restaurateurs at the three venues where England played. At one time an influx of 10,000 Englishmen would only have meant a huge rise in takings. This was certainly not the case in Germany. Compared with the 10,000 Danes who had travelled to the previous Championships in France without any sign of trouble, the England fans' record looks very black.

Politicians are not, generally speaking, interested in football unless it provides publicity for them. Sometimes a minister will attend the Cup Final, but football to most of them is the game that blights our reputation abroad, and it doesn't matter that millions of people get immense enjoyment from it. The governments of many generations have taken huge amounts out of the game in tax money but put nothing back, so now our stadiums compare very unfavourably with the top class continental versions. However, if the football terraces were hotbeds of political activity then the response would be very different.

After the Heysel disaster all obstacles to the extradition of the Liverpool fans were removed by the Thatcher Government. Compare this with the treatment of the Belgian bar owner who shot dead an innocent Tottenham fan who was fleeing from a fight in a bar. The bar owner produced a rifle and fired shots at random, killing this poor fan. In a Belgian court he was given a two-year sentence, but the British Government made no attempt to extradite him to face British justice. And what about the Liverpool fans who had been near-fatally stabbed by the AS Roma fans the year before the Heysel disaster? Did the British Government try to get justice then, or even compensation for these unfortunate fans? In the Heysel stadium, before the trouble and collapse of the wall, the Italians had injured a large number of Belgian riot police at the other end, and one Italian had been arrested for firing a starting pistol. Were he and his pals extradited? There were certainly many who made the accusation that the Italians had started the fighting before the charge by the English fans that led to the tragedy. But all the facts and the search for the truth were lost in the stampede to find a scapegoat. Those people who really wanted to find the guilty men and bring them to justice were conveniently ignored.

The probable advent of membership cards is a classic example of the politicians' wish to control something they don't understand with a simple solution, and also of their keenness to be seen to be doing something. There's trouble in West Germany – right, we'll introduce a membership scheme back in England.

As a regular supporter I can see the reasoning behind the ministers' argument, but not the practical sense of it. Their logic, as far as I understand it, is this: make it so difficult for the hooligan that he will stop attending. The average Joe Public will quit the game under those circumstances long before the yobbo. The problem is that unless the police check every card and also run checks at random then the average hooligan, who is not as thick as everyone imagines, will always be able to get a new card if his is confiscated. (Do you seriously think the hardcore hooligans travelled to Germany on their own passports?)

The issue of membership cards will neither curb violence nor remove the potential for violence. I believe that football fans and hooligans alike will apply for the cards. The people who will be excluded are the armchair or casual fans who attend the occasional match – the guy who takes his son at Christmas or Easter; the group in a pub who decide to go on the spur of the moment; the man who wants to go to see a cup replay two days after his little team have drawn with the First Division's big boys. It won't deter or stop the organised thugs any more than have heavy fines or prison sentences.

Will it prevent a big city club's fans from turning up in their
hundreds for a cup tie, with or without a card? Will it stop
someone exploding into spontaneous violence at a big match
full of tension?

All it means is that smaller crowds will attend during the
regular season, thus requiring less police inside the
grounds – but probably many more outside to make sure
that people are not engaged in card fraud. The police will
also have to make sure that they are not lulled into a false
sense of security, and will still have to estimate which games
will give them the most trouble. It's much harder for the
police to control big crowds outside grounds than inside a
ground, and such a task would be an unnecessary burden for
the police, who would be better engaged fighting violent
crime rather than being asked to enforce a politician's whim-
sical fancy. It's an awfully big hammer to crack a very small
nut. The hardcore hooligan, in any case, is highly unlikely to
fight inside the grounds any more, because of closed-circuit
television. So the net result will be that the young kid who
gets ejected for swearing will lose his card, while the one
who stabs someone three hours before kick-off will remain
untouched.

The only beneficiaries will be the people making money
from producing the cards. The losers, as usual, will be the
average football fan, who will have the dubious privilege of
paying for a government white elephant which will create
another millionaire to be featured in the glossy pages of a
Sunday newspaper supplement. The scheme represents a
ridiculous waste of public money, and it does not address the
real problem. But I have no doubt that, if and when the
scheme is implemented, the minister concerned will pro-
claim it a big success, producing a wealth of statistics to
back up his claims. He will pat himself on the head, move on
to the next thing and forget all about football.

The political theory is that when a membership card

system has eliminated all football violence, then we can apply for reinstatement in European club competition. But the idiots who only turn up for the big match are still in the closet, ready to return for the big European beano. There are plenty, for example, waiting for the 1990 World Cup in Italy. The potential for violence in Italy, should England qualify, is very great. There is, as I have shown, enormous animosity between Italian and English fans. The Heysel tragedy was the culmination of a series of clashes that had been going on since 1980. Young Italians are sure to seek revenge, and the scene will be set for very violent confrontations. If, as hoped, the hooligans drift away from the domestic scene then they will certainly return for the big games in Europe and the World Cup. I do not know the answer to the trouble that occurs abroad, but again I feel sure that the causes lie in the state of the nation at home.

I believe the present blurring of the lines between society and football violence, by politicians and media, makes the future of football uncertain. The game is being used as a scapegoat by authorities who cannot keep law and order. The Heysel tragedy was a horrific loss of life which shocked the football world. Yet the Prime Minister on this occasion displayed how little she understood football by calling on sports writers and other parties to answer this question: 'Why can't the game be played behind closed doors and relayed via television?' It was quite rightly pointed out to her that if this were the case there would be no point in playing the game at all. Anyone with so little understanding of football ought not to be involved in its legislation and control.

Football supporters formed their own association to try to prevent future Heysels, but this has consistently been ignored by both political and football administrators – yet we are asked to believe that they are the experts on football violence. The politicians could yet destroy the game of football as it exists in this country today. Ironically, they could succeed where the hooligans failed.

The very nature of football, with its instant highs and lows, dictates that there will always be outbreaks of disorder, not just in Britain but all over the world. I do not think that we will again witness the sort of crowd trouble inside English grounds that happened in the 1970s, because of the new security-conscious layout of grounds. (Though the Hillsborough tragedy revealed that security-conscious and safety-conscious are two very different things.) But the explosion of violence within our society over the last twenty years cannot be solved by shutting down a few football grounds.

Football is a wonderful game which has given me untold pleasure and will no doubt continue to do so. The era that I have lived through on the terraces also brought me fear and excitement, but I would not have swapped it for anything, and I think the other participants feel the same. It reminds me of the stories I hear about National Service. People who served their term look back on it with affection, and long to recapture the comradeship they experienced at that time. Well, I feel the same way. I also look back with affection at a special period. The only difference is that I had a ball, whereas many people hated National Service at the time. There were times when I was so frightened I would have given anything to be somewhere else, but I lived to tell the tale. I don't think everyone would agree, but it now seems like a golden age, a paradise gone by.

Epilogue

Just about everyone has had their say about football violence: politicians, writers, psychologists and people-watchers. But those who participated in the mayhem have been silent. I have written a hooligan's-eye view, even though I have never been a hooligan in the true sense of the word. I have recorded the facts as I saw them happen. Inevitably some people will say that I am glorifying violence, but I would refute that, and it certainly was not my aim. I do not and cannot speak for the nutters and violent types who have attached themselves to football – the types who went out to hurt people and enjoyed doing it, those who would continue to kick someone who was spark out or repeatedly slash someone with a knife. Nobody knows what makes them tick, and I always tried to keep clear of them. I am thankful that I was never cornered or attacked by that sort; part luck, part sixth sense always kept me one step ahead of them.

As I am a Londoner and an Arsenal supporter, I have obviously reported events with a certain bias, especially about my team. Derogatory remarks and quoted references about other groups of people are not necessarily my own views, but are exactly the way I heard them over the years. Some people reading this will say 'That didn't happen like that,' but that is the way I saw it and remember it. Others will think my behaviour a little anti-social, and indeed I cringe myself at some of the things I did – but most people are a little embarrassed by their teenage behaviour. I am proud that I never attacked or hurt anybody except in self-defence (okay, sometimes I got my retaliation in first!). I will leave the pontificating to the people who earn a living doing just that. I have dealt with the real-life characters and situations that formed my experience. The full story of my seventeen years watching football would dwarf *War and Peace*, so I have confined myself to the parts that gave me the most excitement. I hope I have shared that excitement and communicated something of the complex and colourful world that is the football stadium.

Postscript: Hillsborough

On 15 April 1989 a catastrophe happened which dwarfed all previous football disasters, not just in the number of deaths, but in the horrible way that people had the life crushed out of them, while everyone else was forced to stand by and watch helplessly. The barriers which were put up to control crowds had been instrumental in causing death.

No doubt the existence of rigid secure fencing will be blamed on the hooligans, and the ticketless fans trying to gain entry will take the ultimate rap. Whoever is to blame – and as in most enquiries, the ones who can't speak eloquently and as a unit will probably take the blame – one thing is for sure; the face of football will be changed for ever.

Politicians all shouted loudly the next day, 'We will ban the terraces', but purposely left out the phrase 'We will provide the money'. That means the loser will be the average fan – again. His voice will be lost in the reflex knee-jerk rhetoric, dictated by political expediency. Note the reaction to the *Herald of Free Enterprise* disaster when 'Ro-Ro' ferries were not banned, despite the fact that they are floating accidents waiting to happen.

I hope, though I am far from convinced, that the tragic loss of life will result in two things: firstly, that money is provided to build new stadiums: not lifeless concrete monoliths on the edge of towns, but real stadiums where the fan can feel a part of his football (it is very important that everybody doesn't lose sight of that fact); stadiums with provision for terrace areas, the design being such that the position of the entrances prevents crowd surges. In Brazil, for example, where crowds are far more volatile, they still have large terrace areas.

Secondly, I hope the prevailing voice of common sense as spoken by the average fan will at last be listened to and heeded. For too long he has just been a number to be pushed from pillar to post. Before anyone cries 'hypocrite', remember this: no one ever died from a pitch invasion. If the barriers seen at Hillsborough had been at Wembley in the 1923 FA Cup Final, then thousands would have died (that day tens of thousands forced their way into the ground). Why can't each club have an elected representative from its supporters' club on the board? (I realise that is the 'brave new world' of fans.) Supporters going through the turnstiles provide much more money than TV, yet look at how football is being dictated to by television. Of course, for successful change, politicians must provide football with the will and finance; sadly on both counts they are found woefully lacking .

Why can't we do it like the continentals, and let local authorities own the stadiums, then lease them back to football clubs at a nominal fee? If some big city clubs have to share, then so be it. After all, the Milan clubs can do it, then so can we. Stadiums can be built which enhance spectator safety and still allow the fan to be a comfortable participant. Anything less will be an insult to the dead.

Football has shown it has a capacity for regeneration. It has recovered before from horrific loss of life. But this senseless carnage must never be allowed to happen again. Football's recovery powers are not infinite.